Lumpenbourgeoisie:
Lumpendevelopment

Lumpenbourgeoisie: Lumpendevelopment

*Dependence, Class,
and Politics in
Latin America*

by Andre Gunder Frank

Translated from the Spanish
by Marion Davis Berdecio

Monthly Review Press
New York and London

Originally published as *Lumpenburguesia: Lumpendesarrollo*
by Ediciones de la Banda Oriental, Montevideo, Uruguay,
copyright © 1970 by Ediciones de la Banda Oriental

Library of Congress Catalog Card Number: 72-81764

First Modern Reader Paperback Edition 1974
Second Printing

Published by Monthly Review Press
62 West 14th Street, New York, N.Y. 10011
21 Theobalds Road, London WC1X 8SL

Manufactured in the United States of America

Contents

Mea Culpa   1

Introductory Summary   13

1. Colonial Structure   17

2. Agrarian Structure   26

3. Independence   46

4. Civil War: Nationalism Versus Free Trade   51

5. Liberal Reform   63

6. Imperialism   67

7. Bourgeois Nationalism   75

8. Neoimperialism and Neodependence   92

9. Alternatives and Options   138

Bibliography   146

The discovery of America . . . certainly made a most essential [change]. By opening a new and inexhaustible market to all the commodities of Europe, it gave occasion to new divisions of labour and improvements of art, which, in the narrow circle of ancient commerce, could never have taken place. . . . The productive powers of labour were improved, and its produce increased in all the different countries of Europe, and together with it the real revenue and wealth of the inhabitants. . . . The silver of the new continent seems in this manner to be one of the principal commodities by which the commerce between the two extremities of the old one is carried on, and it is by means of it, in great measure, that those distant parts of the world are connected with one another. . . . To the natives, however, both of the East and West Indies, all the commercial benefits which can have resulted from those events have been sunk and lost in the dreadful misfortunes which they have occasioned.

—Adam Smith (1776)

Gold is the best thing in the world . . . it can even be used to wing souls to paradise.

—Christopher Columbus (1500)

We, the Spanish, suffer an affliction of the heart which can only be cured by gold. . . . I came in search of gold, and not to work the land like a laborer.

—Hernán Cortés (1521)

Where there are no Indians, there is no wealth.
—Franciscan saying (sixteenth century)

Where there is no wealth, the gospel does not enter.
—Bishop Mota y Escobar (seventeenth century)

Let us now see how the distribution of property has divided the population into the various classes which compose the state, established the relations between these classes, and produced the consequences of these relations. Such a study, which is always necessary to an understanding of a country, is particularly indispensable in our case; for our greatest errors are due to our failure to recognize that our society has a unique character and does not resemble in any way the European societies to which we constantly compare it. We have borrowed the terminology of their social organization but we do not possess the substance. . . . When we are told that we have an aristocracy, when we are urged to defer to it and are reminded of the European nobility and the feudal clergy, then we are misled. Words have been foolishly mistaken for realities and an error of language has led to an error of policy. The spell is broken by a simple comparison of those classes with our own. . . . Trade was merely the passive tool of foreign industry and commerce, and its interests were therefore identical. For this reason [the merchants] have a very immediate interest in preserving the unfavorable exchange we are now making and in blocking all efforts to improve the country's present conditions. Today, the cabinets are completely committed to mercantile interests and are deeply interested in keeping us in a state of wretched backwardness from which foreign commerce derives all the advantages. . . . We need a general change, and this change must begin with the material conditions of our society, with these very relations which have, until now, been the cause of our condition.

—Mariano Otero (1842)

Mea Culpa

In their review of nine essays by this author, a group of Mexican critics (Cabral Bowling, Duarte Romero, Escalante Hinojosa, Palma Sánchez, and Rodríguez Escalona) asked how I define underdevelopment. In their "Análisis Crítico," they state:

> Frank suggests a geographic or regional pattern of development and an overly schematic system of transfer of exploitative relationships. We believe that exploitation is a social phenomenon too complex to be explained exclusively in terms of the metropolis-satellite structure, as Frank proposes. . . . His historical analysis *lacks depth*. . . . Would it not be more accurate to state the relations of exploitation in terms of social classes? (Cabral Bowling et al. 1969: 30–33; emphasis in the original)

My answer is affirmative; it *is* more important to define and to understand *underdevelopment in terms of classes*. That is precisely what I have attempted to do in the earlier essays and in the present study, at least insofar as the bourgeoisie is concerned. However, as I maintained in the previous works, and hope to demonstrate more fully here, underdevelopment in a dependent region such as Latin America cannot be understood except as the product of a bourgeois policy formulated in response to class interests and class structure, which are in turn determined by the dependence of the Latin American satellite on the colonialist, imperialist metropolis.

Actually, the intention of my previous work was to emphasize the internal structure of the satellite colony, seen as the historical product of the complex of its relations

1

with the imperialist power; to expose the limitations of the
"development" policies of the "nationalist" bourgeoisie. In
fact, in their explanatory summary of the nine essays, the
aforementioned Mexican critics write that

> the exploitative and contradictory qualities inherent in the
> capitalist system lead Frank to assert that capitalism could
> not exist without the contradictions of a structure of ex-
> ploiter and exploited. Furthermore, this contradiction is
> precisely the cause and the source of the simultaneous and
> dialectically interrelated processes of economic develop-
> ment and underdevelopment. . . . The sociopolitical struc-
> ture reached into the farthest corners of each country. . . .
> In this regard, Frank says: "In the course of the develop-
> ment of world capitalism, Latin American class structure
> has been, basically, the colonial structure imposed and in-
> culcated by Iberian and, later, British and North American
> imperialism. Consequently, Latin America had, and has,
> the class structure of a colonial and neocolonial exporting
> economy, on the local as well as the national level." We
> may conclude that in Gunder Frank's study of underdevel-
> opment, the elements of development, underdevelopment,
> and metropolis-satellite relationships are examined within
> the framework of historical processes within which he suc-
> ceeds in developing his various theses (Cabral Bowling
> 1969: 2ff.).

Apparently, however, in the essays they reviewed, my
success was very relative, since my critics find that the historical analysis lacks depth and the description of the class
structure seems to them an overly schematic, geographic
pattern. It would appear that I have failed in my responsibility to explain my views to my readers. Mea culpa.

A similar failure in communication is evident in the fact
that another writer observes, with satisfaction, that my
book *Capitalism and Underdevelopment in Latin America*

"is an impressive and convincing presentation of the decisive way in which, ever since the Conquest, the destinies of
the Latin American peoples have been affected by events
which took place outside their continent, beyond their
control" (Halperin July 13, 1967: 37). I find it truly remarkable that my book can have persuaded any reader of
the validity of such a view—one which is certainly not my
own. In fact, in *Capitalism and Underdevelopment in Latin
America* particular stress is laid on the fact that

> for the generation of structural underdevelopment, more
> important still than the drain of economic surplus from the
> satellite after its incorporation as such into the world capi-
> talist system, is the impregnation of the satellite's domestic
> economy with the same capitalist structure and its funda-
> mental contradictions. . . . [which] organize and dominate
> the domestic economic, political, and social life of that peo-
> ple (Frank 1967: 10).

Furthermore, in the Preface to the same book, I empha-
sized my conviction that "national capitalism and the national bourgeoisie do not and cannot offer any way out of
underdevelopment in Latin America" (xv). It must be said
that, contrary to Mr. Halperin's impression, dependence
should not and cannot be considered a purely "external"
relationship imposed on Latin Americans from abroad
and against their wishes. Dependence is also, and in equal
measure, an "internal," integral element of Latin American society. The dominant bourgeoisie in Latin America
accepts dependence consciously and willingly but is nevertheless molded by it. If dependence were purely "external," it could be argued that objective conditions exist
which would permit the "national" bourgeoisie to propose
a "nationalist" or "autonomous" solution to the problem
of underdevelopment. But in our view, such a solution

does not exist—precisely because dependence is indivisi-
ble and makes the bourgeoisie itself dependent. We shall
return to this theme in the present study and attempt to
develop it more explicitly, more strictly, and—hopefully—
with greater clarity.

The epigraphs to this study support and illustrate the
three-fold thesis which we will attempt to defend through
an examination of decisive facts in each of the principal
stages of Latin American history, from the Spanish conquest to the present. First, as Adam Smith and even the
conquistadores and their ecclesiastical companions pointed
out, the conquest placed all of Latin America in a position
of subjection and colonial and neocolonial *economic dependence* in relation to the single world system of expanding commercial capitalism. Second, as the post-conquest
ecclesiastics and the Mexican Mariano Otero (in 1842)
also maintained, this colonial or neocolonial relationship
to the capitalist metropolis formed and transformed the
economic and class structure, as well as the culture of
Latin American society, with the transformations in national structure occurring as a consequence of changes in
the forms of colonial dependence. Third, as Mariano
Otero also observed, this colonial and class structure established the very direct interests of the dominant sector
of the bourgeoisie. Using governmental cabinets and instruments of the state, this sector spawns *policies of economic, social, cultural, and political underdevelopment* for
the "nation" and for the people of Latin America. When a
change in the forms of dependence alters the economic
and class structure, changes are in turn produced in the
policy of the dominant bourgeoisie, and these changes,
with a few partial exceptions mentioned below, strengthen
still further the same ties of economic dependence which
gave rise to these policies and which consequently serve to

deepen still further the development of underdevelopment in Latin America. Therefore, concurring with Mariano Otero in his recognition of the fact that "our society has a unique character," although a dependent one, and avoiding a mechanical and literal translation which would result in "an error in language" producing "an error in policy," we may characterize as LUMPENBOURGEOISIE the class which was no more than "the passive [though I would prefer to call it "active"] tool of foreign industry and commerce and its interests were therefore identical" with theirs. The members of this class "are deeply interested in keeping us in a state [or, rather, a process] of wretched backwardness from which foreign commerce derives all the advantages"—a state we may characterize as LUMPENDEVELOPMENT.

This commentary would appear to be particularly timely since Theotonio dos Santos, reviewing my book in his article "El capitalismo colonial, según A.G. Frank," writes:

According to Gunder Frank, underdevelopment is a consequence of the internal contradictions of capitalism . . . which result from the expropriation of the economic surpluses produced by the many and appropriated by the few. Expropriation of this surplus is effected through a chain of exploitations whose strongest link is the center of world capitalism at any given historical period. . . . A second contradiction . . . the metropolis-satellite contradiction, is repeated in the internal economy of the colony. . . . His fundamental thesis, supported with long citations from Latin American writers, is that the colonial economies are designed primarily for exports and are controlled by commercial capital in the national and international metropolis. He demonstrates convincingly, with a wealth of documentation from studies of Latin American anthropology, sociol-

ogy, and history, that the isolation of the Indian is illusory.
. . . He then shows how the Indian's production is exploited by merchants in the metropolis. . . . Frank accounts for these phenomena by relating them to the internal
structure of the colonial country: the pre-eminence of the
export sector and the deficiencies of the internal market
which result from the structure of the export mechanism.
. . . And if a national, industrial bourgeoisie had actually
existed in the past, it has now become increasingly dependent on the capitalist metropolis for financing, marketing,
capital goods, technology, design, patents, trademarks, li-
censes, etc. (dos Santos n.d.: 139–150).

Dos Santos sums up his version of my argument:

It is no longer possible to speak of a progressive national
bourgeoisie. . . . The military coup of 1964 in Brazil was a
reflection of the intensification of dependence brought
about by the alliance of the decadent national bourgeoisie
with foreign capital. A solution to the problem of Brazilian
underdevelopment becomes increasingly remote without
the destruction of the system which has created the problem: the national and international capitalist system (ibid.:
145–146).

It would appear that my thesis requires reformulation
or, at least, some further explanation. In spite of (or beginning with) his explanatory summary of my argument,
which I consider quite adequate, Theotonio dos Santos
concludes his review with a "critique of methodology":

Our principal criticism of Gunder Frank's theory is that he
does not go beyond a structural-functionalist position. . . .
This gives a static character to his argument. The changes
which have taken place, whose importance Frank himself
recognizes, appear simply "irrational," or at any rate merely
the result of fortuitous circumstances, according to his analysis. . . . The first contradiction in Frank's discussion is the

failure to explain why the surplus produced and remaining in Latin America is invested in any given way . . . (ibid.: 146–147).

In another study, dos Santos writes that

the parameters of a "liberated" Latin America are determined by the remnants of a colonial exporting system. This is so, not only because a large proportion of our surpluses are carried off, as Frank believes, but fundamentally because our socioeconomic structures were dependent ones. . . . We believe we have clarified this basic question. . . . It is not a problem of satellization, as Frank believes, but rather of the reinforcement of certain kinds of internal structures which are conditioned by a situation of international dependence (ibid.: 44–45).

In the aforementioned "critique of methodology," dos Santos concludes:

The colonial pattern which Frank outlines cannot be combined with class analysis, as he seeks to do. . . . As for changes in the system, it is not enough to demonstrate the persistence of the colonial structure. It is necessary to explain how the forms of dependence have changed, in spite of its persistence. For these changes have produced the profound contemporary crisis, which both requires and facilitates a socialist solution (ibid.: 150, 148).

This was, in fact, my intention, both in *Capitalism and Underdevelopment in Latin America* and in the collection of essays entitled *Latin America: Underdevelopment or Revolution*. Since both volumes were written more than half a decade ago and both have provoked sharp criticisms (the previously mentioned Mexican appraisal as well as dos Santos's, among several dozen less severe reviews), I feel that instead of discarding the methodology or rejecting the thesis, I should attempt to strengthen the methodology and clarify the dialectic relationship between the actors and their changing setting. This I propose to do in the present essay. In order to define the character of the principal actor and the nature of the setting, it may be appropriate to name and identify both—with perhaps a touch of poetic license—LUMPENBOURGEOISIE and LUMPENDEVELOPMENT.

If this writer "does not make a profound historical analysis" and if this essay is an interpretation *rather than a history* of Latin America, it is because I prefer to leave that task to the professional historians—I am not one—and because here I wish only to assist, insofar as I am able, the forces of the people by distinguishing between deceptive, dangerous, bourgeois reformist strategies and a revolutionary strategy which is truly popular. I am aware that in so limiting the objectives of the present study, I shall have failed to fill in the more serious gaps in my previous work, that is, an analysis of the conditions of the nonbourgeois classes and a proposed strategy of class struggle. The need for the latter is demonstrated not only by this study but also by other writers and by the Latin American reality as well.

In order to anticipate certain additional criticisms, I would like to make another confession: like certain of my critics, I have thus far been unable to liberate myself from the cultural colonialism which imposes upon us a terminology (and with it, perhaps, an approach) that is erroneous and inconsistent with the reality we analyze so that we may change it. In using the word "dependence," I adopt (temporarily, I hope) the new fashion which has become equally acceptable to bourgeois reformists and Marxist revolutionaries by virtue of widespread usage. That is to say, the term "dependence" lacks a specific, well-defined content. In this essay I attempt to give "dependence" an operational definition, as Reichenbach would say. However, I am aware, and hope that the reader will be especially sensitive to the fact, that today the word "dependence" is no more than a euphemism that cloaks subjection, oppression, alienation, and imperialist, capitalist racism, all of which are *internal* as well as external. This racism is a burden to the impoverished peoples and—as a Frantz Fanon or a Jesus Christ might say—will be an affliction to the exploiter and the oppressor as well, until the oppressed free themselves and, thereby, their enemy. I have been told that I ought never to use the word "bourgeoisie" because it denotes a social process which has never existed and will never exist in colonial and neocolonial Latin America. But I have been unable to replace it with another term. I find "dominant class" unsatisfactory; "oligarchy" has even more ambiguous implications in connection with the Latin American reality; and I cannot even consider "aristocracy" or "middle class," which are terms used by the ideologists of imperialism and their Latin American counterparts. Thus, I have chosen to retain "bourgeoisie" and to add "lumpen" to it. Finally, I continue to use the word "underdevelopment," a word whose etymological origins and present usage is the most shameless negation—ideological, political, economic, social, cultural, and psychological—of an accurate conception of reality. I am unable to find a substitute for this word, to free myself from this cultural colonialism. In order to make a start at replacing this word with a term which mirrors reality, if not perfectly then at least more accurately, might we not look to Adam Smith, the scholar who provided us with one of the epigraphs to this essay and who was concerned with colonialism and colonies? Might we not designate the consequences of colonialism as "lumpendevelopment"?

One more mea culpa: owing to its origins, this study

perhaps lacks the consistency which it should have. It is
the last of several versions prepared as lectures or earlier
essays. It began as a class which the Students' Center of
the Department of Sociology of the University of Chile
kindly asked me to give to inaugurate the academic year in
April 1969. After minor revisions, it was published in *So-
ciología* (No. 2, 1969) under the title: "Estructura colonial,
estructura de clases y responsabilidad del sociólogo." I
made extensive revisions of this version for the Congress
on Latin America, held in July 1969 in Jyväskylä, Finland,
where I gave two lectures which were subsequently published in Finland under the title "Dependencia económica,
estructura social y subdesarrollo en América Latina." The
final section of this version, which deals with the present
period, was published in revised form, in Spanish, as
"CEPAL: Política del subdesarrollo," in *Punto Final* (Santiago, Chile, Suplemento de la edición No. 89, 14 octubre
1969) and in English as "The Underdevelopment Policy of
the United Nations in Latin America" in *NACLA News-
letter* (Vol. III, No. 8, December 1969). I revised the study
extensively once more for oral presentation on the occasion of the Fifth Meeting of the Departments and Schools
of Economics in Latin America, held in Maracaibo, Venezuela, from November 3 to 10, 1969, which I was honored
to attend as a special guest to deliver the one lecture. I presented this version of the study at the Centro de Estudios
Postgraduados of the Facultad de Ciencias Económicas y
Sociales of the Universidad Central of Venezuela in Caracas, where I was invited to deliver a series of lectures to the
Seminar on Economic and Social Development and Integration in Latin America. In written form, and titled "Dependencia económica, estructura de clases y política del
subdesarrollo," I presented the expanded essay as a paper
at the Ninth Latin American Congress on Sociology, held

at the Universidad Nacional Autónoma de México, from November 21 to 25, 1969. At the same time, I submitted it as a contribution to the first issue of a journal published by the Department of Sociology of the University of Chile, where I work as a teacher and researcher and where these ideas were discussed at length, criticized, and refined by my students.

Finally, with the help of the above-mentioned and other criticisms and reviews of my earlier publications; with my experiences at the lectures I delivered and the criticisms of my listeners, of other participants at the congresses, and of friends; with the contributions of my colleagues and—most especially—my students in the Department of Sociology, I once again revised and enlarged the essay considerably, adding the Preface for the present version. Having very nearly exhausted the possible variations on the theme with the previous titles, I decided to use them only as an explanatory subtitle for the present essay, since I feel that this is an appropriate moment for a new title. However, I would not care to claim exclusive paternity for this title, nor do I know if anyone else would care to do so.

My intellectual debts concerning this essay are thus many, though rather impersonal and undefined. Nevertheless, my responsibilities, or rather my faults, are entirely my own. I hope that the lengthy process of gestation and baptism through which this version, as distinct from the earlier ones, has passed will have served to eliminate some of the flaws of language and communication that were found in its predecessors.

Since I have not yet finished the long-promised study—more extensive and possibly more intensive—of the effects of "dependence" on the means of production and agrarian lumpendevelopment in Latin America, and especially Mexico (though some parts of the study are included in the section on agrarian structure in the present book, while others remain in a longer manuscript on Mexico drafted and put aside more than three years ago), and since I cannot say when I will finish it and write the dedication, I would like to dedicate this small study to my Mexican son, Miguelito, whose own development has been most contradictory and dialectical, and to others like him who are now trying to find their bearings.

—A.G.F.

Santiago, Chile
December 21, 1969

Introductory Summary

This study will sustain a three-part thesis by means of an examination of the determining factors in each of the principal stages of Latin American history. The three parts of the thesis are:

I. The Conquest placed all of Latin America in a situation of growing subjection and *economic dependence*, both colonial and neocolonial, in the single world system of expanding commercial capitalism.

II. This colonial and neocolonial relationship to the capitalist metropolis has formed and transformed the economic and *class structure*, as well as the culture, of Latin American society. These changes in national structures have occurred as a result of periodic changes in the forms of colonial dependence.

III. This colonial and class structure establishes very well defined class interests for the dominant sector of the bourgeoisie. Using government cabinets and other instruments of the state, the bourgeoisie produces a *policy of underdevelopment* in the economic, social, and political life of the "nation" and the people of Latin America. When a change in the forms of dependence modifies the economic and class structure, this in turn generates changes in the policy of the dominant class which further strengthen the very same bonds of economic dependence which produced the policy and thus aggravate still further the development of underdevelopment in Latin America. There are a few exceptions to this process which will be discussed presently.

In this study we will examine these determining relationships between (I) economic dependence, (II) class

13

structure, or lumpenbourgeoisie, and (III) policy of under- or lumpendevelopment, as they affect each of the following topics: (1) the colonial structure, (2) the agrarian structure, (3) Independence, (4) the civil wars: nationalism vs. free trade, (5) the liberal Reform, (6) imperialism, (7) bourgeois nationalism, (8) contemporary neoimperialism and neodependence.

1. The colonial and class structure is the product of the introduction in Latin America of an ultra-exploitative export economy, dependent on the metropolis, which restricted the internal market and created the economic interests of the lumpenbourgeoisie (producers and exporters of raw materials). These interests in turn generated a policy of under- or lumpendevelopment for the economy as a whole.

2. The agrarian structure and agrarian means of production are transformed, at given moments in the history of the various countries, in response to the commercial opportunities and, above all, to the fluctuations in foreign demand for agricultural products. We will give special attention to the cases of Barbados, Mexico, Chile, and Cuba.

3. The Independence movement in Latin America was the product of the economic interests of the producers of raw materials for export, who had grown strong under the free trade regime at the end of the eighteenth century and had seized the political opportunity provided by the Napoleonic Wars. The desire for political independence, in order to increase still further its capacity to export raw materials to the burgeoning British metropolis, led the Latin American bourgeoisie to choose an economic policy which increased economic dependence and, with it, the development of underdevelopment.

4. Nevertheless, the policy of underdevelopment could not be effectively implemented until the sector of the bour-

geoisie most intimately associated with the production and marketing of raw materials subjugated, by political and military means, the more industrial and, therefore, more nationalistic sector of the bourgeoisie in the civil wars of the nineteenth century. The decision in favor of free trade was one of the principal policies of lumpendevelopment employed by the Latin American lumpenbourgeoisie to promote its own economic interests. This policy increased dependence on foreign powers and reinforced the structure of underdevelopment in Latin America.

5. The liberal Reform of the last century was not simply the result of ideological enlightenment, but also of the economic interests of the bourgeois exporters of agricultural products. These reforms took place at different times in each country, but it would appear that in each case reform occurred after a conspicuous increase in the production and exportation of these products.

6. When imperialism accelerated the production and exportation of raw materials in Latin America at the end of the nineteenth century, the economic and class structure of the various countries was once more transformed. The Latin American lumpenbourgeoisie became the junior partner of foreign capital and imposed new policies of lumpendevelopment which in turn increased the dependence on the imperialist metropolis.

7. Bourgeois nationalism and twentieth-century industrial development in the principal countries of Latin America both represent the political response of the Latin American bourgeoisie to the changes in the national economic structure produced by the crisis in the imperialist metropolis that was caused by the two world wars and the economic depression of the 1930s. The great reduction in the volume of Latin American exports and/or imports which the crisis produced set the stage for a policy of in-

dustrial development in Brazil, Argentina, Mexico, and, on a smaller scale, in Chile, Colombia, etc. However, this development was limited by the class structure of the lumpenbourgeoisie—a legacy of the earlier period of dependence—as well as by the recovery of the imperialist metropolis, which began in the 1950s.

8. The development of neoimperialism has meant neodependence for Latin America and a new transformation of the contemporary economic and class structure. The Latin American bourgeoisie, which now includes an industrial sector, is once more the junior partner of imperialism and favors policies which increase subjection and dependence and renew the development of lumpen- or underdevelopment. For the people of Latin America, a policy of real development requires revolutionary strategy and socialism.

1. Colonial Structure

In order to understand the origins of the colonial structure of Latin America, we must examine the reasons why Latin America is underdeveloped today while North America is developed, though both began as European colonies. Two sorts of interrelated, hypothetical explanations have been proposed. One of these is that North America benefited by the transplantation of the progressive institutions of British capitalism while Latin America was handicapped by the establishment in the New World of the regressive institutions of decadent Iberian feudalism. The other, a related explanation derived from Weber's *The Protestant Ethic and the Spirit of Capitalism,* suggests that an important difference in character existed between the settlers of North America and Latin America: the former were enterprising Protestants and the latter lazy Catholics. The first of the two explanations must be rejected because it is clearly lacking in historical validity. Capitalism first developed in Catholic Italy, Spain, and Portugal, and the institutions of the Protestant British colonies in the South of the United States and the Caribbean were not noticeably more progressive than those of Latin America. Furthermore, it is incorrect, as we shall see below, to assert that the institutions of the Iberian peninsula were transplanted to Latin America. With regard to the second explanation, if real differences actually existed between the settlers of the various regions of the New World, an inquiry into the reasons for these differences would be necessary.

In the epigraphs to this study, the motives of the Spanish colonizers were described in the words of the conquer-

17

ors and the clerics who accompanied them. Adam Smith summarized these motives when he wrote in *The Wealth of Nations*: "All the other enterprises of the Spaniards in the new world, subsequent to those of Columbus, seem to have been prompted by the same motive. It was the sacred thirst of gold that carried Oieda, Nicuessa, and Vasco Nugnes de Balboa, to the isthmus of Darien, that carried Cortez to Mexico, and Almagro and Pizzaro to Chile and Peru" (Smith 1937: 529). How were the gold and silver mines of Mexico and Peru exploited? Clearly, by exploiting the Indians and manipulating their high civilization and great social structure. It is equally clear that the Spanish and Portuguese did not organize the exploitation of mines in the Caribbean, Brazil, Argentina, and other areas on a similar scale only because of the absence of mines in these regions. The failure of the English who settled in North America to work mines of precious metals was due to the very same circumstance; there were no such mines to work. Why did the Portuguese, the French, and the British establish sugar plantations in Brazil and the Antilles and cotton plantations in the South of the United States? Because, although they could not work mines in these regions, the climate did permit them to develop an export economy, exploiting slave labor which could be imported from Africa. We may now ask why these same French and English did not do likewise in New France and New England. The answer is self-evident: because these regions lacked the geological and climatic conditions and the indigenous population necessary for the establishment of an export economy. This was the case in Argentina, as well, until the development of the world capitalist system made it possible, in the nineteenth century, to develop the region as an exporter of wool, meat, and wheat, while São Paulo, parts of Colombia, Costa Rica, etc., became coffee exporters.

Thus, a comparative study of the varieties of European colonies established in the New World leads us to a fundamental conclusion which may at first seem paradoxical, but is nevertheless an accurate reflection of the dialectic of capitalist development: the greater the wealth available for exploitation, the poorer and more undeveloped the region today; and the poorer the region was as a colony, the richer and more developed it is today. There is only one basic reason for this: underdevelopment is the result of exploitation of the colonial and class structure based on ultraexploitation; development was achieved where this structure of underdevelopment was not established because it was impossible to establish. All other factors are secondary or derive from the basic question of the type of exploitation. This applies as well to the type of settlers who populated the various regions and to their activities.

In North America—or, more precisely, in northern North America, which differed from the cotton-growing South—a diversified economy of small agricultural holdings and small industries was established from the outset. A similar society existed for a considerable time in various parts of Latin America. As Guerra y Sánchez has said in *Sugar and Society in the Caribbean*:

> The process of the allotment and division of Cuban land during the sixteenth, seventeenth, and eighteenth centuries led to the creation of a class of large-scale and small-scale proprietors who were descended from the first settlers and who were deeply attached to their native soil. They were mainly a poor, rough people who lived in isolation from the outside world . . . but in Cuba the foundations were laid for a new and original nationhood, the fruit of three centu-

ries of settlement. The different systems of allotment and utilization of the land determined the different destinies of the British and the Spanish Antilles: for the one, decline; for the other, progress, slow but constant (Guerra y Sánchez 1964: 35–36).

This progress lasted, we might add, until they too became sugar plantations in the nineteenth century. In Colombia, according to Nieto Arteta,

> until the middle of the last century, manufacturing and the rich agriculture of Oriente contrasted with the indigence of Occidente and the poverty of the Central region, the departments of Boyacá and Cundinamarca. In Occidente, mining . . . in Boyacá and Cundinamarca, the latifundium. . . . In Oriente the situation was quite different. . . . There are no latifundia; there could be none. No mines of gold or silver were found. Therefore, the negro was not brought in. . . . Manufactures were developed. . . . The economy of eastern Columbia, in the period we are discussing, was not oriented to the foreign market (Nieto Arteta 1969: 79–80).

In Central America, "Costa Rica, the poorest and most isolated province of that period . . . had a more homogeneous social structure, composed almost exclusively of the descendants of Spaniards" (Torres Rivas 1968: 16). So it was in many other parts of Latin America, especially in what is now the relatively less underdeveloped *Cono Sur* (Southern Cone) and in the British colony of Barbados. However, in the latter the social structure did not survive for very long, as Harlow notes in his *History of Barbados*, citing contemporary observers:

> In the days when a variety of small crops were grown, the land was occupied in small holdings by a large number of tenants. This system, usual in most young British colonies, was partly the result of the original grants of small allot-

ments to the first settlers. . . . In this way the island was possessed of a numerous and sturdy "yeoman" class, who were indeed the backbone of the colony. With the arrival of the sugar industry, this healthy condition of affairs was altered. Sugar planting to be successful requires large acres of land and a plentiful supply of cheap labour: the Dutch system of long credits provided the more affluent with means to obtain both. But the small planter with his few acres and little capital could not face the considerable initial expense of setting up a sugar factory. The land in consequence fell more and more into the hands of a coterie of magnates. . . . An example of the process was to be found in Captain Waterman's estate, comprising 800 acres, which at one time had been split up among no less than forty proprietors. . . . Emphasizing the same fact . . . is the land value belonging to Major Hilliard. Before the introduction of the new manufacture (in about 1640), the plantation was worth 400 pounds; yet in 1648 half of it was sold for 7,000 pounds. . . . By 1667, Major Scott said that, after examining all the records of Barbados, he found that since 1643 no less than 12,000 "good men" had left the island for other plantations and that the number of landowners had decreased from 11,200 smallholders in 1645 to 745 owners of large estates in 1667, while during the same period the negroes had increased from 5,680 to 82,023. Finally, he summed up the situation by saying that in 1667 the island "was not as strong, although it was forty times richer than it had been in 1645." This two-fold process, whereby a sturdy English colony was converted into little more than a sugar factory owned by a few absentee proprietors and worked by a mass of alien labour, constitutes the main feature of Barbadian history (Harlow 1926: 40–44, 306–310).

The regions of Latin America which are today the most backward—parts of Central America and the Caribbean, the Northeast of Brazil, the areas in the Andes and in Mexico where the indigenous population predominates,

and the mining zones of Brazil, Bolivia, and central Mexico—have in common the fact that in the early period
(and, in many cases, in the present as well), they were the
areas where the exploitation of natural, and to an even
greater extent human, resources was most extreme. This is
a characteristic feature of an export economy.* And this
dreadful misfortune, as Adam Smith called it, is shared
with many parts of Asia and Africa, despite the many cultural differences which separate these regions, and despite
the fact that, in some, the development of world capitalism
totally transformed the indigenous social structure, while
in others—Cuba, for example—the development of world
capitalism completely transformed the social structure
which the Europeans themselves had previously established there. Consequently, the degree and type of dependence on the metropolis of the world capitalist system is the
key factor in the economic and class structure of Latin
America. As Aldo Ferrer observes in his study of the Argentine economy:

> Mining, tropical agriculture, fishing, hunting, and lumber
> were the expanding activities that attracted capital and

---

* In developing my thesis regarding the most intensively colonialized
and exploited regions, in order to include Asia and Africa as well as
Latin America, I designated them, in my statement in Caracas, as
"ultra-underdeveloped." Compañeros Francisco Mieres and Héctor
Silva Michelena objected, maintaining that, in accordance with my
"theory," ultra-underdevelopment should be characteristic of regions
where contemporary rather than past colonialism assumes its most extreme forms. Thus, according to Silva, the most ultra-underdeveloped
country in Latin America is Venezuela. I considered the theoretical ob-
jection valid and agreed that Venezuela is indeed a case of ultra-underdevelopment, thanks to the ultra-exploitation caused by the boom in oil
exports. We agreed to designate this boom, very provisionally, as an
example of the "active" development of ultra-underdevelopment and to
find another term for the "passive" state of ultra-underdevelopment in
the exporting regions of earlier periods in the development of world
capitalism.

labor. . . . Associated with export activities were the wealthy property owners and merchants, together with high officials of the Crown and the clergy. . . . These sectors . . . were the internal colonial market and the source of capital accumulation. . . . As the small groups of property owners, merchants, and political figures acquired more wealth, they bought from abroad more manufactured consumer and durable goods. . . . There is little doubt that both the structure of the export sector and the concentration of wealth were fundamental obstacles to the diversification of the internal productive structure, which would have led to a rise in technical and cultural levels and the emergence of social groups interested in developing a domestic market, as well as export items not controlled by the metropolitan market (Ferrer 1963: 19–21).

The bulk of the capital available for investment was channeled, by the institutions of underdevelopment, into mining, agriculture, transport, and commercial export enterprises linked to the metropolis; almost all the rest went to luxury imports from the metropolis, with a very small share left for manufactures and consumption related to the internal market. Because of commerce and foreign capital, the economic and political interests of the mining, agricultural, and commercial bourgeoisie were never directed toward internal economic development. The relations of production and the class structure of the latifundia, and of mining and its economic and social "hinterlands," developed in response to the predatory needs of the overseas and the Latin American metropolis. They were not the result of the transfer, in the sixteenth century, of Iberian feudal institutions to the New World, as is so often and so erroneously alleged.

This does not mean that the colonial and class structures were static. On the contrary, the constant changes in the former occasioned corresponding transformations in the latter, as the fate of manufacturing in the colonial period demonstrates. For example, the economic depression in Spain in the seventeenth century, which reduced the shipping tonnage between the mother country and New Spain to one-third of what it had been in the sixteenth century, made possible a significant development of local manufacturing. Before the close of the eighteenth century, the textile industries alone employed 60,000 workers in Mexico (Orozco and Florescano 1965: 73). The Viceroy of New Spain wrote in 1794 that

> with no help of any kind, or direct protection by the government, they have progressed enormously; to such a degree that one is amazed by certain types of manufactures, principally cottons and cloth for rebozos. The coarse wools also provide raw material for many factories. . . . In these domains it is very difficult to prohibit the manufacture of those things which are made here. . . . The only way to destroy such local manufactures would be to send the same or similar products from Europe, to be sold at lower prices. This is what has happened to the great factory and guild which existed for all sorts of silk textiles, now barely remembered; and much the same fate has befallen the factories manufacturing printed cloth. . . . The decline of the [Acapulco] trade was quite natural in view of the changes which have taken place, the growth of European factories, and the generally inferior quality of Oriental cloth. Since the year 1789, there has been a steady increase in the textiles and spices that have been imported (Revillagigedo 1966: 191–192, 200, 203).

The Chilean historian Hernán Ramírez Necochea (1967: 65) points out that "it is extremely important to emphasize that this occurred in various countries in America. 'Free trade,' writes the Peruvian historian Carlos Deustúa Pimentel, 'brought in its wake the destruction of the few factories that were flourishing and supplied the American markets with goods of all sorts.' " Referring to the situation in the province of La Plata, Ricardo Levene notes: "It was, in effect, the active trade that began with the *Reglamentos* of 1778 which caused the decline of the first national industries." The transformations in the Latin American social structure which were produced by changes in colonial relations are equally evident in the agrarian structure.

2. Agrarian Structure

Let us examine the economic and social structure of the rural sector of colonial society and study the growth of latifundia and the principal methods of agricultural production.

We will look first at the case of sixteenth-century Mexico. There, the early period was marked by the enslavement of the Indian, which lasted from 1521 to 1533. This was followed by the *encomienda*—a system under which the Indian was obliged to provide labor or tribute to the *encomendero*. After a short time the labor *encomienda* was eliminated (although in colonial Chile it persisted for a long time and was impossible to extirpate). Between 1545 and 1548, there was a great epidemic which reduced the available labor supply at a time when the discovery of silver increased the demand for laborers. As a result of the increased need for labor and the diminished supply, the *encomienda* system was increasingly altered until it became what was called *el catequil.* (In Peru it was called *la mita;* the system was never established in Chile because it did not suit Chilean needs.) It lasted until about 1630, but after 1580 it was no longer the dominant method of utiliza-

---

This chapter summarizes some of the conclusions reached as the result of a research project in which the seminar I lead is engaged. This project is concerned with the ways in which changes in the forms of dependence have affected and continue to alter the agrarian structure and methods of agrarian production, particularly on the latifundia, in a number of Latin American countries (only a few of which are mentioned here). It is hoped that this research will result in the publication of one or several studies that will be more complete than the tentative views presented in this chapter.

tion of labor. The predominance of the latifundium or hacienda, which increased after 1580, began as the result of another epidemic which further reduced the available labor supply, and consequently production in the mines as well. Prices for agricultural products increased, and agriculture became a much more profitable activity than it had been previously. At the same time, the profits of mining diminished, in both absolute and relative terms, in comparison with agriculture. There was therefore a transfer of capital from mining to agriculture at a time when depopulation had reduced the efficiency of the small, native agricultural producer. Under such circumstances, the Mexican hacienda became a predominant institution—and with it came peonage, which was later termed feudal. In other words, the modes of production which were employed and then replaced in Mexico—or never took hold at all in Chile—and the resulting transformations in the class structure responded to changes in the colonies' ability to serve metropolitan needs. Once they had achieved predominance, the *hacendados* were able to impose—through the *cabildo* (city council) and the viceroy—the policies which suited them with regard to prices, indenture, vagrancy laws, etc.*

Throughout this period, the nature of the agricultural structure and the changes it underwent were determined by the colonial status of the region. This is confirmed by its most distinguished observer, the German geographer Alexander von Humboldt, who, in 1811, wrote in his famous *Political Essay on the Kingdom of New Spain*:

Traveling along the ridges of the Andes, or the mountainous part of Mexico, we everywhere see the most striking ex-

---

* This paragraph is a summary of an unpublished 130-page manuscript by the author.

amples of the beneficial influence of the mines on agriculture. Were it not for the establishments formed for the
working of the mines, how many places would have remained desert? How many districts uncultivated in the four
intendancies of Guanaxuato, Zacatecas, San Luís Potosí
and Durango? . . . Farms are established in the neighbor-
hood of the mine. The high price of provision, from the
competition of the purchasers, indemnifies the cultivator for
the privations to which he is exposed from the hard life of
the mountains. Thus, from the hope of gain alone . . . a
mine which at first appeared insulated in the midst of wild
and desert mountains, becomes in a short time connected
with the lands which have long been under cultivation
(Humboldt II: 407–408).

At the end of the eighteenth century, Count Revillagigedo, Viceroy of New Spain, remarked in his *Instrucción
Reservada* (1794) to his successor that

far from a decline, in the years of free trade there was a
considerable increase in the volume of goods and merchan-
dise introduced as well as in the amount of wealth and
produce extracted. In these regions, there has been great
progress in recent years; the export of products has nearly
tripled in comparison with earlier years and consists princi-
pally of hides, dyes, cotton, Campeche wood [*palo de tinte*],
and myrtle, and above all, the precious cochineal. Tanned
products, soap, cotton, and flour were sent from these domains to Havana and the islands, where they were needed
in agriculture. . . . The harvests of grains of all kinds have
increased greatly in these domains. . . . The division of
land is much more [un]equal than it is in Spain; there are
several industrious men who own enough land to establish
an entire kingdom. . . . In the last few years, the output of
the mines has increased considerably. . . . This increase has
not been due to great bonanzas or to greater purity of the
metals; it is due primarily to the increased numbers of peo-

ple working in the mines. . . . Many former merchants, accustomed to high profits and low risks in the overseas trade,
turned to agriculture and mining when they realized that
the new commercial system would allow them lower profits
and entail higher risks" (Revillagigedo 1966: 198, 202, 205,
209, 210).

The contemporary historian Enrique Florescano writes
that

> from 1779 to 1803 the value of the tithes, which reflects the
> upsurge of agriculture, almost tripled. . . . For the first time
> the value of agricultural production (which was calculated
> on the basis of the value of the tithes) exceeded the value of
> mining activities, in spite of the fact that the height of min-
> ing prosperity was from 1779 to 1803. . . . When Humboldt
> visited New Spain in 1803, he was able to confirm that the
> increase of wealth in the last thirty years of the eighteenth
> century had aggravated the economic inequalities in colo-
> nial society. . . . In a word, the rise in prices had made the
> great landholders richer; the division between the prelates
> and the parish priests was deepened; and the situation of
> the poor became more intolerable. . . . The growth of the
> haciendas caused the displacement of a great number of
> rural laborers and the impact of the cyclical crises in-
> creased. The number of unemployed rose and social tension
> in the cities grew. The inequalities caused by the great in-
> crease in wealth were so dramatic that, in commenting on
> the situation which prevailed from 1803 to 1807, Humboldt,
> Fray Antonio de San Miguel, Abad y Queipo, and the lib-
> eral group writing in the *Diario de México* predicted the
> outbreak of social conflict. In September 1810, after thirty
> years of continuous rise in prices, after the crises of 1785–
> 1786 and 1801–1802, and precisely when another infla-
> tionary wave reached its peak, Hidalgo initiated the revolu-
> tion which was to make New Spain an independent country
> ten years later (Florescano 1969: 193–195).

It should be remembered that Independence was not achieved under the humble auspices of Hidalgo and Morelos but with the *Plan de Iguala,* sponsored by the *hacendados* and their representative, Iturbide. Nonetheless, this important event in Latin American history (which was to repeat itself under surprisingly similar circumstances in Mexico in 1857 and again in 1910) illustrates our central thesis that changes in the relationships of colonial dependence alter the economic and class structure in Latin America. In this case, the changes were brought about by the Bourbon reforms, which permitted greater freedom of trade after 1778, and by the growth of demand in Cuba for Mexican flour as a result of the sugar boom which, in turn, was caused by the Haitian revolution of 1790, a reflection of the French Revolution of 1789. We shall see this process repeated when we study the causes of Independence; it is an example of the way in which this transformation, in its turn, produces changes in the class policy of the dominant groups and, thus, in the struggle of the oppressed class.

The same pattern is analyzed by Mario Góngora in *El Origen de los "inquilinos" de Chile Central*:

In the eighteenth century, a major change took place; it was a consequence of the trade in wheat with Peru which produced a more intensive organization of the hacienda and a revaluation of the land from Aconcagua to Colchagua— both exporting regions. The change consisted of an increase in land rentals, with the payment to the landowner becoming an increasingly important factor. The dependence of the tenant farmers increased and their duties became more onerous. . . . The great hacienda filled its need for service from the ranks of the tenants. The term *arrendatario* [tenant, lessee], which was also applied to men of middle and high economic levels, fell into disuse, and the term *inquilino* acquired special significance. In short, rural holdings, from leases to peonage masked as *inquilinaje*, assumed forms that were entirely unrelated to the *encomienda* and the other institutions of the Conquest. These holdings have their origin in the second period of colonial history, a period marked by stratification: the landholders moving upward, the poor Spaniards and various categories of racial mixtures (*mestizaje*), downward. . . . Stratification increased in the eighteenth and nineteenth centuries, and as it did the condition of the *inquilino* deteriorated. In the eighteenth century his position was one of increased dependence; a process of proletarianization of the *inquilino* had begun and was accelerated in the nineteenth century (Góngora 1960: 114–115).

The initial period of this process, at the end of the eighteenth century, coincided with the Independence movement, as we shall see below.

A similar process was at work in Cuba, according to the "Discurso sobre la agricultura de la Habana y medios de fomentarla," which the principal Cuban agriculturist and thinker of the period, Francisco de Arango y Parreño, drafted for the King of Spain in 1792. In this document he referred to all "those who know nothing about agriculture in America, nor of its order and progress . . . which will seem impractical and ridiculous to many," but he understood and explained, better than anyone, the true nature of the entrepreneurial, if not capitalist, mode of agricultural production.

In 1763 Havana was still in a state of near infancy; yet by 1779 it was a great commercial center; it sent large shipments of wax to New Spain, supplied the Peninsula with all the sugar it needed and procured abroad, produced many raw hides, some coffee, the tobacco needed by the *Real Factoría*. . . . The resurgence of Havana may be dated from the unfortunate War of 1760. Its tragic surrender to the

English served to revive it in two ways: first of all, a single year of trade with Great Britain served to flood the country with considerable wealth, a large number of blacks, tools, and textiles; and second, it demonstrated the importance of this trade to our Court and called a great deal of attention and concern to the question. . . . The facts were incompatible with the monopoly of the *Compañia*. They constituted a mortal blow; they stripped away its oppressive privileges; free and open trade between Havana and Spain, with moderate tariffs, began to operate; a monthly mail service to communicate with the metropolis was established and a contract for the importation of blacks was concluded with several firms. . . . Other unforeseen factors combined with these providential measures to favor the agriculture of Havana. Heaven unleashed on France the scourge which afflicts it today. The resulting confusion and disorder in its colonies diminished their production and increased the value of ours, thus preventing the abundance of blacks provided by the aforementioned *Real Cédula* of 1789 from having injurious effects. Today, in the improved situation created by the misfortunes of our neighbor, we sell our sugar at extremely good prices; but what will happen tomorrow? This should be the real concern for the island of Cuba. . . . From all this, it may be inferred that if the government wishes to develop industries in its colonies and enjoy favorable trade balances, it must emulate the political course of other nations: it must compare the costs of each branch of the agriculture of other countries with similar costs in its own colonies, examine the costs of freighting and shipping these products to their markets and, if the comparison proves unfavorable to us, then we must reward, grant tax exemptions, in a word, concern ourselves with raising our economy and industry to the level of our rivals instead of levying taxes, imposing restrictions, and devising obstacles. . . .

Let us examine the obstacles, with examples from the

case of sugar. . . . First obstacle: tools and blacks cost them less. The different degree of prosperity and vitality which the French and English have achieved in trade and the arts makes it possible for their colonists to obtain tools and other necessities at better prices than we are able to get. This is a well-known advantage which no one would attempt to deny. The same applies to blacks; we have only recently made it possible to buy them in our colonies with some degree of ease, and even now, how much more needs to be done to make it possible to actually satisfy our needs? Second obstacle: they spend less on maintaining them and get more work from them. The English, French, and Portuguese have, on the whole, the same system for feeding their slaves. They give them neither money nor food (although they are obliged, by law, to provide the latter); they provide only a small parcel of land for them to cultivate and allow only the time judged adequate in each case. We grant an equal amount of time for whatever farming they choose to engage in, but without limiting the daily ration of meat and soup. The English and French have fewer holidays and consequently get more work from their slaves. Third obstacle: their greater skill in agricultural techniques. This fact does not require proof. It is not necessary to walk through the fields of Cuba to realize that here the very names of such useful knowledge as Natural Physics, Chemistry, and Botany are unknown. Even dispensing with these aids, one need only stop to observe at any point, and one is aware of the different state of one agriculture from the other. Fourth impediment: they operate their factories with greater efficiency and economy. . . . There is not a single windmill or watermill, nor even the notion of what these things are, while in the foreign colonies, not only are these things very commonplace, but, besides, the places where these devices are impractical are provided with well-constructed iron sugar mills. They place crossbars and beams almost horizontally and are able to grind a greater quantity of cane in the same time. Furthermore, to boil the juice of the cane, they use reflectors which save them an immense amount of wood, and thus they are able to manage with only the dry waste of the cane [*bagazo*], while in Havana we are still discussing the relative merits of these reflectors as compared with an outlay of one-ninth of the value of the harvests and cutting down an entire mountainside of trees for each sugar crop. Fifth obstacle: their movements are freer and more protected. . . . Sixth obstacle: their tariffs encourage industry instead of retarding it. Seventh and final obstacle: unlike ourselves, they are not burdened by the enormous weight of usury. The greater part of the haciendas of Guarico and Jamaica belong either to merchants or to absentee owners who live in the metropolis. In either case, they are immune to the double tyranny of the tradesman, since they are not obliged to borrow money at interest in order to make the heavy investment necessary before each harvest nor do they have to pay high prices for indispensable staples. Blacks, machines, tools, and even cloth to clothe their slaves are sent to them from the metropolis, either by the owner himself or the friendly merchant. Thus, the scarcity of cash is of small importance to them. In Cuba, on the other hand, there is no owner in the metropolis or assistance from the merchant and, furthermore, the greater part of the landowners establish their haciendas with very little capital. They go into debt to build them and find themselves at the mercy of the moneylenders and the merchants who deal in the goods they need. The results may be observed in the frequent and ruinous business transactions in Havana. Let us reflect upon these obstacles. If we do not surpass the industry of our rivals in any respect, if at every point of the comparison I have just outlined the distance between our ways and theirs is as great as the distance from ten to one, how will we dispose of our surplus, after relieving the present shortage caused by the disaster of Guarico? How can we continue to trade in foreign markets? . . .

Seize the opportunity to bring to our own land the wealth which the small territory of Guarico gave to France. This thought will seem ridiculous and impractical to those who know nothing of agriculture in America, nor of its order and progress. Accustomed as they are to the slow pace of change in Europe, they seem to think that the establishment of a sugar mill or a cotton or coffee plantation, etc. needs as many years before producing as the mulberry groves of Granada and that the labor necessary to produce these crops will be provided by the gradual reproduction of the species. My only reply is to recommend the study of history to them. There they will see the growth of Jamaica in a very few years, the establishment in French Santo Domingo, in less than thirty years, of the great fund of wealth it possessed before the insurrection of the slaves, and they will see how we, without as much assistance, developed our agriculture to its present level in only sixteen years—from 1763 to 1779.

Anyone who knows something about this type of plantation would agree with me in saying that if there were wealth enough to purchase (and license to introduce into Cuban ports) in just one year all the blacks needed to cultivate this land, then, within three years production would be twice as great as that of the French part of Santo Domingo, if we are to believe what our *Gaceta* tells us. There is no doubt of it: our era of happiness has arrived. . . . What are we waiting for? What is stopping us? (Arango y Parreño 1965: 184–197)

In fact, they did not wait, nor did anything stop them. With Arango y Parreño as their leader, the Cubans carried out a program whose results were analyzed by Manuel Moreno Fraginals in his masterful study: *El Ingenio: El Complejo Económico Social Cubano del Azúcar.*

Between 1763 and 1792 all the obstacles to the development of Cuban sugar production were eliminated and the Island became the largest producer in the world. . . . It is important to emphasize that the great sugar boom of the second half of the eighteenth century was made possible by the extremely high prices for the product, which prevailed for a period of more than sixty years. In 1748, sugar was priced at 12 to 18 *reales* in the port of Havana. In 1760, the price was from 12 to 16. With very slight variations, these averages were maintained until the French Revolution, when the market, upset by the ruin of Haiti, reached fabulous highs of 36 and 40, only to return to the normal range of 13½ to 16 at the close of the century. The average harvest, before the fall of Havana to the English, involved an area of 320 *caballerías** under cane cultivation. Thus, the average area of the sugar mill in 1762 was from 10 to 12 *caballerías,* while in 1792 it can be estimated at about 22 *caballerías.* *The process of expanding the productive capacity of the sugar mill also served to double the amount of land under cane cultivation.*

The boom of 1792 was characterized by the remarkable extent to which all activities not directly or indirectly related to sugar were abandoned. . . . In what José Sedano called "neglect of the necessary in order to promote the profitable," . . . the *vegueros* (small tobacco planters) were the first to feel the savage impact of the expansion of sugar production. It was to be expected that the tobacco lands would be the first to be taken over by sugar cultivation. They are fertile, naturally irrigated, sufficiently cleared to be given over immediately to cane cultivation; they include the woods needed for the fires required in processing cane; they are well located and have roads leading to the ports of embarkation (tobacco was also an export crop); and, finally, *they are in the only populated areas where wage labor could be found for work on the sugar mills.* Thus, initially the growth of the sugar mills followed the paths marked by the

---

* A *caballería* is a West Indian land measurement equaling about 34 acres.

tobacco plantations . . . the eleven best tobacco plantations which José de Coca put to the fire belonged not to him
but to the tobacco planters. Over the smoking fields and the
burning tobacco huts, plantings of sugar cane spread and a
sugar mill grew: *Nuestra Señora de las Mercedes*. Its owner:
José de Coca. . . .

All this wild speculation, which enriched the oligarchy of
Havana still further, had terrible effects on the lower
classes. By the middle of 1799, the captain-general was obliged to admit that prices had risen in a scandalous fashion
and that the bread sold in Havana was made with maggoty
flour. The report of the newly arrived Marqués de Somerue-
los was impressive. The most difficult situation was to be
found in the mills themselves. Because of the war, there was
a shortage of jerked beef and dried codfish. The undernour-
ished blacks were forced to work twenty hours a day and
died by the thousands in the fields. Dr. Francisco Barrera y
Domingo, who witnessed this period of annihilation, left
terrible descriptions of the Cuban canefields in 1797. In his
discussion of the diseases suffered by the blacks, he observes that the fundamental cause of illness was malnutri-
tion and that without the *guarapo* (fermented cane liquor)
and the cane itself, "they would surely die of hunger." . . .

Naturally, none of these things could have happened
without complete official support. . . . The sugar boom of
1792 made all administrative and legal procedures in the
colony outdated. Changes which ordinarily would have
taken place in the course of several decades, occurred in a
few years. However, it is important to note that by becoming a sugar government, *the oligarchy accelerated Cuba's
passage to capitalism and were obliged to effect such significant changes in the colonial superstructure that they must,
of necessity, go down in history with the well-deserved title of
great reformers*. . . . "Capitalist production creates an appropriate landholding system of its own, and thus feudal
landholdings and small peasant holdings combined with the
communal system were all converted into a form (with in-

ternal, legal variants) which suited this system of production." This process, described by Marx, was at times more manifest in Cuba than in the countries of Europe, and in the scant twenty years of the rise of sugar cultivation, an entire juridical system was liquidated (Moreno Fraginals 1964: 5, 10, 11, 12, 13, 35, 37; all emphasis in the original).

This was the beginning of the historic process of the development of underdevelopment in Cuba. Change in the form of dependence, transformation of the economic and class structure, a new political bourgeoisie (all affecting the superstructure as well)—this was described in 1928 by Ramiro Guerra y Sánchez in a chapter entitled "The Inexorable Evolution of the Latifundium: Overproduction, Economic Dependence, and Growing Poverty in Cuba," in his classic work, *Sugar and Society in the Caribbean.* Essentially, the same pattern of growth of the latifundium emerged during the same period in Argentina, Uruguay, São Paulo, Chile, Peru, Colombia, Venezuela, Central America—in all of Latin America. Since we cannot, in this essay, examine the process in each of the countries, we will confine ourselves to the case of one country which provides us with a particularly instructive example: Mexico.

Turning to the Mexican experience of the late nineteenth and early twentieth centuries (when, as a result of penetration by expanding North American and European imperialism, demand for the products of Mexican agriculture and mining increased), let us examine the evidence of authoritative contemporary witnesses—men who were later to become Under-Secretary of State and Director-General of Agriculture, respectively, in Madero's government.

The agrarian policy of the dictatorship was broadly outlined in the early period by Minister Pacheco who, like

Díaz, was a general of humble origins. Its final form as a
component of a capitalist economy was described by Minister Molina, a powerful Yucatan landowner with lumber
concessions in Quintana Roo and a politician who was
closely associated with the *científico* group. Both of these
men subscribed to the capitalist axiom that the key to progress is the growth of public wealth. They believed that to
achieve this growth, peace was indispensable—"at any
price," as the traitor Huerta said. Pacheco revived the old
composiciones de demasías which had played such a large
part in the establishment of latifundism. With the law of
December 15, 1883, he created the surveying companies,
encouraged land speculations, and provoked a great rise in
the value of rural property. In a short time, a large number
of latifundia were established, and the popular *caudillos* of
the Díaz revolution, along with a large number of foreigners, formed a landed aristocracy. At the same time, the
Church quickly recovered its former power by purchasing
haciendas through intermediaries or inheriting them from
the dying, who were terrified by visions of hell's fires. . . .
Daily, the consequences of this policy became more evident. Larger harvests were gathered every year, land values
rose and labor costs fell steadily, and the wretchedness of
the poor deepened as the wealth of the landowners increased. Thus, capitalist organization proved to be the most
effective method of increasing the enslavement and poverty
of the people and aggravating the inequalities that existed
between the poor and the rich. It has been said, correctly,
that the increased income from the land makes capitalist
agriculture a flagrantly profitable enterprise, thanks to the
rise in price of agricultural products and the reduction of
production costs, both of which derive from the enslavement of the agricultural laborer and the control of the government by the landowners—a control which, in addition,
provides them with the weapon with which to overcome the
small landholder. The cultivation of the monopolized land

with enslaved labor produced large returns, and as income rose the increase itself became an incentive to further exploitation on a capitalist basis . . . the monopoly of the land leads inevitably to a reduction in wages. . . . For this reason, we have stressed very low wages as one of the factors which promote capitalist exploitation of the land by reducing the cost of production and consolidating the system. The banking system became an openly privileged source of unquestioned political and social power. . . . The railroads were effective tools in the consolidation of the latifundia and agrarian slavery. . . . The achievement of the dictatorship of General Díaz consisted in the systematic organization of a capitalist regime (González Roa and José Covarrubias 1917: 86–88, 55, 56, 71).

The Director-General of Agriculture, Lauro Viadas, a well-known *científico,* confirms the foregoing in his *Informe Oficial*:

The persistence of large properties is the logical consequence of the development of agriculture in our country. They will continue to endure for the same reason, in spite of the firmest and most well-intentioned measures, so long as we are unable to eliminate the obstacles to our agricultural progress. Large-scale agriculture becomes pre-eminent, eliminating small family farming and absorbing the land; it is attracted, and I venture to say powerfully attracted, by the economic advantages provided by two circumstances. The first of these is the high price brought by articles of prime necessity, due to the low volume of our agricultural production and the high duties levied on goods from abroad, which we are forced to import in order to supply our needs. The costliness of these products results in high profits for the landowners and subsequently increases the value of cultivable land, thus rendering it available only to capitalist enterprises. The second circumstance is the low cost of labor, which reduces the cost of production in relative, if not in absolute, terms and for this reason results in increased profits in agriculture. A third factor must be added to these two, which are the principal bases upon which our agriculture rests. Although this third element is in a sense the natural consequence of the first two, it is nevertheless in itself an extremely significant obstacle to the achievement of the *desideratum* of the small holding—we refer to the absence of a group of noncapitalist farmers who have the resources necessary for family farming. The effects of our inadequate agricultural production are doubly unfortunate. On the one hand, high prices penalize consumer groups by raising the cost of essential articles, while on the other, these high prices naturally attract capital to agriculture, making the participation of the small farmer in agricultural enterprises doubly difficult. So long as the capitalist finds agriculture profitable, it is as absurd to think of the possibility of small family farming as it is to suppose that the workers in a cottage industry can compete with a large manufacturing enterprise or to believe that a small commercial establishment might reduce the large importing firms to bankruptcy. It would undoubtedly be possible, in a few cases, for the small farmer to coexist alongside the wealthy landowner; just as a modest industry might survive beside the great factories. But these isolated cases, which occur only under special local conditions, could never be reproduced on a national level in industry or agriculture (Viadas 1960: 112–113).

History has demonstrated the accuracy of this analysis —even after the Revolution, in which two million lives were lost, and after the most profound and extensive bourgeois agrarian reform in this hemisphere. A recently published book, *Neolatifundismo y Explotación* by Rodolfo Stavenhagen and others, notes the following:

The impact of foreign demand is clearly discernible in the following figures: in 1940, the value of the production of livestock and agricultural products amounted to about 10.3 percent of total exports, while in 1945 the figure was nearly 21 percent. This would appear to indicate that since then, conditions in foreign markets have been of greater significance than internal conditions in determining growth in agriculture and stock-raising. This meant that the best irrigated lands, credits, and inputs were channeled into agriculture for the external market, while the country suffered shortages of corn, beans, vegetable fats, and other necessities, which had to be imported; and black markets, which were the source of more than a few fortunes, appeared (Stavenhagen, et al. 1965: 75–76).

Since 1940 and, more concretely, after 1946, (1) the development of agriculture depended more on external factors (demand and the provision of inputs) than on internal ones; (2) the best lands—irrigated lands—and other resources such as capital, labor, credit, and physical inputs became concentrated in particular regions and in the hands of a few owners; (3) this growth opened the door to foreign capital, which began the process of gaining control of the nation's agriculture; (4) agricultural products, as exports, became the base of Mexico's commercial balance; . . . (5) the country's economic policy—more concretely, its fiscal and monetary aspect—supported the monopolization of land and the exploitation of human labor, instead of improving the wretched conditions endured by the rural population and liberating it from exploitation; (6) this same policy became a factor in producing grave inequities in the distribution of income (77–78).

These tendencies were aggravated in the past decade. The rate of agricultural development was maintained at a high level until 1955, as a result of the opening of large, irrigated areas to cultivation and the increase, already noted, in the levels of investment by the public, as well as the private, sector. Encouraged by rapid and inflationary development, [investors] earmarked a substantial part of their resources for crops that were suited to large-scale production. Thus, "encouraged" by the Korean War, the international market held steady and offered attractive prices for the principal export crops: cotton, coffee, and tomatoes (78–79).

It is therefore very important to emphasize that the *minifundio* really includes 86 percent of the units under cultivation. . . . *This is the central problem in agriculture today* (84; emphasis in the original).

The 1960 census showed 1,031,000 holdings in production. Of these, 94.3 percent obtained income of less than 25,000 pesos, while at the other extreme, 2 percent of the holdings absorbed 70.1 percent of the value of sales. In order to clarify the extent of concentration in agriculture, it should be noted that in the United States, 10 percent of the agricultural holdings produce 40 percent of the sales, and it is believed that even this represents a high degree of concentration. The foregoing makes it clear that agriculture is a magnificent undertaking for a few, while the great majority of the population engaged in this activity lives in precarious conditions. More than 55 percent of the holdings counted in the census reported sales of less than 1,000 pesos [$80] in 1960 (86–87).

The total population engaged in agriculture rose by 33 percent between 1959 and 1960. In the same period the number of *ejidatarios* increased by only 9 percent and the number of proprietors fell by almost 5 percent, as a result of the process of concentration of land in the private sector. Consequently, the number of salaried laborers in agriculture increased from 2 million to 3.3 million. This means that in 1960 the landless rural population was greater, in absolute terms, than it was in 1930, and also in 1910. Today this group constitutes more than half of the total agricultural population. Analyzing the entire period under consideration (1930 to 1960), we note that, given an increase of 70 percent in the total agricultural population, the number of *ejidatarios* has increased by 100 percent, the number of landholders by 113 percent, and the number of landless agricultural laborers by only 33 percent. Furthermore, considering only the period from 1940 to 1960, the proportions are reversed. In these two decades, the agricultural population as a whole increased by 60 percent. While the number of *ejidatarios* grew only by 22.6 percent, the increase in landholders was 81.6 percent and that of landless agricultural workers, 74 percent. These figures reflect the change in the government's agrarian policy after 1940 (30–31).

The traditional hacienda has, for all practical purposes, disappeared from the national agrarian scene, with the exception of certain remote regions of Chihuahua or Chiapas. But the great holding, which monopolizes land, water, and other resources to the detriment of the small farmer (private as well as *ejidatario*), continues to be the rule rather than the exception in many parts of the country. In order to evade agrarian legislation, the large holdings are apparently subdivided and registered in the names of relatives of the landowners or "fronts." In this way new latifundia have been established, especially in the rich, irrigated zones of the Northeast. For example, in the Yaqui Valley, 85 proprietors control 116,800 hectares of the best irrigated land, which is registered in the names of 1,191 individuals; that is, the size of each property averages 1,400 hectares. There are no statistics which would enable us to quantify this phenomenon, but a reading of denunciations by peasants in all parts of the country makes it evident that neolatifundism is much more widespread than the census figures would seem to indicate (Stavenhagen: 19).

One cannot avoid concluding with Stavenhagen and his fellow authors that

the agrarian problem in Mexico is more complex and, in certain respects, undoubtedly more serious than it was when the *Ejército del Sur* entered the struggle, under the leadership of Emiliano Zapata, more than half a century ago. The concentration of land and other productive resources has assumed new forms and has combined with increased foreign control, exercised by enterprises like Anderson, Clayton and Company, to constitute a single fact—the growing exploitation of enormous masses of peasants. . . . Neolatifundism is not an isolated phenomenon, nor can it be attributed to circumstantial factors: the wiles of a *latifundista,* the dishonesty of a government official, the shortage of resources or trained personnel in a given government agency. Neolatifundism is simply the natural consequence of the existing power structure, that is, the class structure of the country (back cover, 19).

This conclusion, reached by investigators whose specific concern is contemporary Mexican agriculture, is precisely the thesis which the present study proposes to apply to all of Latin America and to its history—until the Cuban Revolution.

3. Independence

We have anticipated historical events, and now we must return to the eighteenth century to examine the causes of formal Independence in Latin America. In the first place, it is noteworthy that Independence came precisely in the period (from 1810 to 1820) when the Napoleonic Wars had weakened the colonial ties between the Spanish and Portuguese metropolises and their American possessions and when the Napoleonic armies had actually occupied the parent states. This change in the colonial relationship, which was to alter the social structure of Latin America, was the culmination of a long, historic process, begun years before. Since the destruction of the Spanish Armada by the English in 1588 and the economic colonization and de-industrialization of Portugal by means of a series of commercial treaties which culminated in the Methuen Treaty of 1703, Great Britain had virtually eliminated the Iberian countries from participation in world capitalist development. The process was exemplified by the exchange of English textiles—an industrial product—for Portuguese wines—an agricultural product: this trade agreement was made famous by Ricardo, who used it to justify the exploitation of Portugal by England on the basis of a supposed natural law of comparative advantage. England, and France until the defeat of Napoleon by the British, had gradually achieved complete control of Spanish and Portuguese trade and colonies.

In a futile attempt to resist the inevitable historic development and to recover a larger portion of the trade for themselves, Spain and Portugal liberalized their commercial regulations with respect to their colonies during the period of the Bourbon reforms of the late eighteenth century. But it was too late. The measures only swelled the tide they were intended to stem. As the Viceroy of New Spain pointed out in 1794, the increase in trade resulted in an increase in the production of raw materials for export and in the profits they produced in Latin America. It also fortified the economic and political power of the bourgeoisie which produced these raw materials in Latin America, while the deluge of cheap manufactures (also noted by the Viceroy) from the metropolis—and, through it, from its Asian colonies—overwhelmed the local manufactures which had flourished in many parts of Latin America during the seventeenth-century depression in the metropolis. Thus when the political crisis in the metropolis provided the opportunity, certain sectors of the creole bourgeoisie hastened both to seize power and the economic advantages which derive from political control of economic and social policy. This "reform," if such it can be called, was also the result of changes in colonial relations which had produced modifications in the local economic structure as well as in the interests and policies of the creole classes.

Luis Vitale summarizes the process in his *Historia de Chile*:

The basic cause of the Revolution of 1810 was the existence of a social class whose interests conflicted with the system of domination imposed by the metropolis. This social class was the creole bourgeoisie. At the end of the colonial period it controlled the principal sources of wealth, but the government remained in the hands of the representatives of the Spanish monarchy. This contradiction between economic power in the hands of the creole bourgeoisie and political power monopolized by the Spaniards is the motivating force which set the revolutionary process of 1810 in motion. The interests of the local bourgeoisie conflicted with those of the Spanish empire. While the former needed to find new markets, the Spanish Crown restricted exports to suit the convenience of Peninsular trade alone. While the creole bourgeoisie wished to buy manufactured goods at lower prices, the Empire restricted them to consumption of articles which Spanish merchants sold to them at high prices. While the Americans requested a reduction of taxes, Spain imposed new ones. While the native bourgeoisie demanded that the accumulated capital and economic surplus remain in Latin America, the Spanish empire took a large part of the surplus and the floating capital. The creole bourgeoisie aspired to the seizure of power because to govern meant to control the customs house, the repository of goods controlled by the Crown, fiscal revenues, high government posts, the army, and the state apparatus which formulated laws on the taxation of imports and exports. Transfer of power would not bring a transformation of society. The local bourgeoisie simply wanted to assume control of the aforementioned business of the Crown. This is the reason for the essentially political, formal character of the Independence movement (Vitale 1969: 156–157).

It would be an error to consider the economic demands separately from the rest of the creole bourgeoisie's class aspirations. The driving force of the 1810 Revolution was the complex of demands by a bourgeoisie determined to seize power, to achieve self-determination, and to control both economic power and the political power vested in the state apparatus. They viewed such control as the sole guarantee of fulfillment of their needs as a class. The creole bourgeoisie was aware that the colonial system barred them from access to the political power that was the key to a new economic policy designed exclusively for their benefit. The number of creoles in high positions in the army, the Church, and public office is irrelevant. What is important is that the creole bourgeoisie as a class was not in power. The structure of the colonial state definitively closed the path of power to them (165).

The truth is that the men who led the 1810 Revolution were, in the main, of bourgeois social origin. In Argentina, the creoles Saavedra, Castelli, and Pueyrredón were *hacendados;* Vieytes, Lezica, and Matheu were wealthy merchants. In Paraguay, the struggle was led by *mate* producers and tobacco growers, like Yedros and General Cabañas. In Uruguay, the cattlemen of the coast, among them Artigas, and the merchants engaged in contraband trade with the English and French and led the struggle for independence.* In Venezuela, the most distinguished leaders, Miranda and Bolívar, were the sons of powerful landowners. In Chile, landholders, mine owners, and the wealthiest merchants led the 1810 movement. The most distinguished leader of the 1810–1811 period, Juan Martínez de Rozas, was the richest man in the colony—a merchant, landowner, and lawyer (166).

The liberal philosophy of the eighteenth century, which fathered the bourgeois-democratic revolution, was used in Latin America to attain only one part of this revolution: political independence. The European bourgeoisie's arguments against feudalism were adapted by the creoles in the struggle against the Spanish monarchy. In Europe, liberal philosophy was the doctrine of the industrial bourgeoisie; in Latin America, it was the ideology of the landholders, the mine owners, and the merchants. The vocabulary of liberalism was used in the service of different class interests. While in Europe liberalism served as an instrument of the industrial bourgeoisie against the landowners, here it was utilized by the landholders and mine owners against the Spanish monopoly. There it served the cause of industrial protectionism; here, the interests of free trade (171–172).

---

* It should be noted that although we are substantially in agreement with Vitale's views, as quoted above, we cannot agree with his estimate of Artigas, whose historic role was, in reality, the contrary of what Vitale's remarks imply. With regard to Artigas, we must also acknowledge as a shortcoming our failure to discuss his career and its significance in the chapter on nationalism and free trade.

As in so many other cases in Latin American history, changes in colonial relations which were initiated overseas produced changes in the structure of the creole class, and this in turn led to revisions in the policies of the dominant sector of the local bourgeoisie. In this case, it led to the struggle for "independence." In the long run, these policy revisions served to confirm the shift to a new set of colonial relationships; that is, they reinforced the ties of economic dependence by strengthening the export economy and the structure of underdevelopment. However, this did not occur automatically; it was the result of the imposition of the class policy of that sector of the Latin American bourgeoisie which emerged victorious from the civil wars. After independence was won, the diverse economic, social, political, and ideological forces—each in pursuit of its own interests and image—sought to control the future of the people of Latin America who were, as a result, subjected to lumpendevelopment.

4. Civil War: Nationalism Versus Free Trade

In 1824, the British Chancellor, Lord Canning, said: "Spanish America is free, and if we do not mismanage our affairs, she is English." History was to prove him right, but the "management" was not so automatic or rapid or easy as the chancellor might perhaps have desired. In order to fulfill Canning's hopes and, later, the hopes of the U.S. Secretary of State and father of Pan-Americanism, James Blaine, it would be necessary to assure the cooperation of the Latin American bourgeoisie. But, as another European, Guizot, informed the French Chamber of Deputies:

> There are two great parties in the countries of South America: the European party and the American party. The less numerous of the two, the European party, includes the most enlightened men; those who are most familiar with the ideas of European civilization. The other party, closer to the soil, imbued with purely American ideas, is the party of the land. This party seeks to develop the region through its own efforts in its own way, without loans, without relations with Europe . . . (quoted by Astesano 1960: 15).

For half a century the two parties struggled for control of the state and for the decision as to which of the two policies would prevail. The "European" party, which favored the closest possible relations of dependence on the European metropolis, and which therefore had firm political and military support from that quarter, was represented by the "most enlightened" spokesmen, from Moreno and Belgrano, by way of Rivadavia, to Sarmiento and Mitre. These men are considered national heroes in Argentine history since they were finally successful in imposing their

51

philosophy and their policies of dependence. As early as 1810, in his famous *Representación de los Hacendados,* Moreno expounded the policy based on the exportation of agricultural and livestock products. Almost fifty years later, in his *Facundo,* Sarmiento savagely criticized the provincials, who were still incapable of appreciating European "civilization." His class, the producers and exporters of raw materials, had fought for "independence" in order to enjoy this "civilization," yet other sectors of that society continued to block the path to complete fulfillment of this policy of civilization or—as their present-day heirs would call it—"development."

Because they were ultimately defeated, history barely records the names of the "American" spokesmen and statesmen of the provinces of La Plata: Drs. Francia and López, father and son, in Paraguay; Agüero, Yáñiz, Ferré, and perhaps even Rosas in Argentina. Their "American" policy was not as rooted in the soil or the countryside as Guizot believed. Its roots were in the interests of the provinces, which sought protection for local industries struggling against the ruinous competition imposed upon them by the "European" policy of the cattle-raising exporters. Paraguay adopted the most extreme version of the "American" policy. Paraguay was the first to win independence, but it refused to join the Argentine Republic. "If Dr. Francia had not succeeded in isolating Paraguay, there is no doubt that this beautiful country would today be a poverty stricken annex of the poverty stricken Argentine provinces," said the French consul in Buenos Aires, in 1836 (quoted in Cardoso 1949: 76). In isolating his country from relationships which would result in dependence of foreign countries, Dr. Francia and his successors, the Lópezes, achieved a Bismarckian or Bonapartist type of national development that differed from all other Latin

American countries of the period. They built a railroad with domestic capital; they developed national industries by engaging foreign technicians but prohibiting foreign investment, as the Japanese were to do many years later; they established free, public, elementary education—almost eliminating illiteracy, according to contemporary sources; and furthermore, with the help of the Guaraní Indians, they expropriated the great latifundia and merchant enterprises. Theirs was the most popular government in America. When this "American" policy—which became distinctly expansionist by the middle of the century—came into conflict with the aspirations of the "European party" in Buenos Aires, Montevideo, Rio de Janeiro, and Europe itself, Paraguay was defeated in the War of the Triple Alliance, in which six-sevenths of its male population was annihilated. Thereafter, Paraguay was opened to "civilization."

In Argentina, the *federales* of the provinces battled the *unitarios* of the port of Buenos Aires and, at times, the "federalism" of Rosas in the province of Buenos Aires, which was a producer of agricultural exports. The *federales* opposed the "European" trade policy, which favored ever greater freedom of trade. They used arms and they advanced arguments like Yáñiz's, which held that

> it would be foolhardy to compare native industry with English. These enterprising manufacturers have already sent us greatcoats (which are an important product of the industries of Córdoba and Santiago), wooden stirrups of the kind we use here, woolens and cottons which are superior to our lightweight cloth, heavy flannels and linens from Cochabamba that are cheaper as well. They have ruined our factories completely and impoverished the large numbers of men and women who depended on spinning and weaving for their livelihood (in Astesano 1960: 49).

Agüero said: "Crafts, industry, and even agriculture, itself, in these regions would be reduced to the most complete neglect and abandonment; many of our provinces would inevitably be ruined" (quoted in Astesano 1960: 49 and Rosa 1943: 38–39). Brigadier General Pedro Ferré, perhaps the most active of the "Americans," argued:

> I believe that free trade is fatal to the nation. I shall never be able to understand how restrictions on trade could constitute an obstacle to industry. . . . Of course, a small number of wealthy men would suffer, because they would be deprived. . . . For the less wealthy classes, there would be little difference . . . but, on the other hand, the condition of entire towns of Argentinians would begin to be less wretched and we would not be bedeviled by the knowledge of the frightful poverty, with all its consequences, to which they are condemned today (Ferré 1921: 371–372).

Although pressure from the federalist and provincial groups succeeded in establishing a protectionist policy during part of the Rosas period, the protection it provided was neither adequate nor decisive. Shortly after the defeat of Rosas at the battle of Caseros, the new government lowered tariffs again. Under Mitre, however, Buenos Aires still did not have complete control of the provinces. This was not achieved until the governments of Roca and Pellegrini, after 1880. Nevertheless, by mid-century, a partisan of the "American" position commented:

> After 1810 . . . the country's balance of trade had been consistently unfavorable, and, at the same time, native merchants had suffered irreparable losses. Both wholesale export trade and retail import commerce had passed into foreign hands. The conclusion seems inescapable, therefore, that the opening of the country to foreigners proved harmful on balance. Foreigners displaced natives not only in

commerce but in industry and agriculture as well (quoted in Burgin 1946: 234).

As Burgin correctly analyzes in his study of Argentine federalism,

> the economic development of postrevolutionary Argentina was characterized by a shift of the economic center of gravity from the interior towards the seacoast, brought about by the rapid expansion of the latter and the simultaneous retrogression of the former. The uneven character of economic development resulted in what was to some extent a self-perpetuating inequality. The country became divided into poor and rich provinces. The interior provinces were forced to relinquish ever larger portions of the national income to Buenos Aires and other provinces of the East (Burgin 1946: 81).

To sum up: for a century "the economic life of the country revolved around one great master wheel, which is export trade," as the Argentine minister of the treasury remarked when this wheel suddenly stopped turning, after 1930. It should be noted that not only the structure of production but the entire "development policy" of the Argentine bourgeoisie—tariffs, taxes, monetary and foreign exchange policy, incorporation of new lands into agricultural production and distribution of these lands among large landowners, immigration of new labor supply, policy regarding wages, ports, railways, and other sectors of the infrastructure—was shaped by its determination to revolve in this sterile circle which developed the contemporary underdevelopment of Argentina, its neighbor Uruguay, and, in fact, all of Latin America. Australia (another "new" country, like Argentina), which also began to export wool, meat, and wheat a century ago, did not inherit a class structure like Argentina's. Apparently, as a result of the discovery of gold there in 1858, a working class evolved which proved able to oblige the government to adopt effective policies of protectionism and rural immigration for reasons of self-interest rather than "development." It was these policies which later made development possible in Australia.*

We have given particular attention to the case of Argentina because it is perhaps the most spectacular example of the struggles which raged throughout Latin America in the half-century following formal independence. In Mexico, for example, Esteban de Antuñano rejected the

> doctrine of the English writer which holds that we Mexicans should devote ourselves exclusively to the cultivation of our land, because we have an abundance of land of very good quality, and leave to the foreigners the task of supplying us with all kinds of cloth and the various manufactures . . . of all nonagricultural articles because they could do this without competition. . . . The ultimate result of such a policy would be to eliminate all of our workshops (Antuñano 1957, II: 157).

The liberal Antuñano and the conservative Lucas Alamán in establishing the beginnings of a sizable textile industry in establishing the beginnings of a sizeable textile industry in Puebla and Orizaba, equipped with the most advanced textile machinery of the period. This industry replaced the old-fashioned manufactures which had been virtually destroyed, both by free trade and by the Wars of Independence. As a stimulus to the new industry, Alamán founded the Banco de Avío to provide financing. However, by the end of his term as minister, he lacked the political support

---

* I owe this comparative interpretation to David Seymour, who advanced these views in an unpublished essay when he was a student of mine.

that would have guaranteed the long-term success of his work. Other farsighted Mexicans of this period defended the national cause and would probably have been called "Americans" by Guizot or "barbarians" by Sarmiento. Perhaps it is not accidental that, like Antuñano, who was born in Veracruz, and Alamán, a native of Guanajuato, all the great men came from the provinces and none from the "Europeanized" capital. This includes such men as Lorenzo de Zavala of Zacatecas, José Maria Luis Mora of Comonfort (educated in Querétaro), Ponciano Arriaga of San Luis Potosí, Benito Juárez of Oaxaca, and, finally, Mariano Otero of Guadalajara, who wrote the lines we have used as an epigraph for this essay, observing, among other things, that:

> Trade was merely the passive tool of foreign industry and commerce, and its interests were therefore identical. . . . Today, the cabinets are completely committed to mercantile interests and are profoundly interested in keeping us in a state of wretched backwardness from which foreign commerce derives all the advantages. . . . We need a general change, and this change should begin with the material conditions of our society, with these same relations which have, until now, been the cause of our condition.

However, in spite of the accurate analysis which many of these "Americans" made of the way in which dependence determined class structure, and the latter in turn resulted in a policy of underdevelopment, and in spite of their keen desire to replace this policy with a policy of development, the very same economic, social, political, and ideological forces they studied were responsible for the fact that by the middle of the nineteenth century sufficient power to establish a genuine policy of development did not exist anywhere in Latin America. On the contrary, in all of Latin America the struggles between "Europeans" and "Americans" ended with the definitive victory of the former—the heirs of "Independence." This was so because throughout the colonial period, dependence had denied the "Americans" the strength they needed to achieve a level of development that would have enabled them to impose such a policy in the post-Independence period. Instead, the "European" lumpenbourgeoisie built "national" lumpenstates which never achieved true independence but were, and are, simply effective instruments of the lumpen-bourgeoisie's policy of lumpendevelopment.

The United States had a very different experience. There was a long struggle (which culminated in the Civil War of 1861–1865) between the industrialists and nationalists of the North, who demanded high tariffs and the incorporation of the Far West into national institutions under national control and, opposing them, the "Europeanized" Southerners, who favored free trade and sought to extend slavery to the West. Southerners produced cotton for the industries of Europe—which gave them the same support they gave to the "enlightened" partisans of the European position in South America. But, as we observed at the start of our study, the settlement of northern North America did not involve the same type of colonization and dependence as did South America's; conditions for this type of exploitation did not exist in the North. Consequently, the class structure which developed there, based at the start on small farmers, did not present any obstacle to a development policy which permitted the Northern bourgeoisie to become strong enough to use independence to promote integrated development, to defeat the planter/exporters of the South in the Civil War, to impose a policy of industrialization and arrive at their own industrial "take-off" point and, finally, to arrive at the period of imperialism and neoimperialism.

After winning the war against the producers of raw materials and the free-traders of the South, the victorious General Ulysses S. Grant commented:

> For centuries England relied on protection, carried it to extremes, and got good results from it. There is no doubt that it is to this system that that country owes its present power. After two centuries, England has found it desirable to adopt free trade because protection no longer offers advantages. Very well, gentlemen, the knowledge that I have of my country leads me to believe that within two hundred years, when America has gotten all that she can get from protection, she too will adopt free trade (quoted in Santos Martínez 1961: 185).

Although Grant miscalculated future developments by one hundred years, he did understand the past and his own time very well. It was not accidental that the free trade movement began in Manchester, when that great textile center had reached the highest level of industrial development achieved in that period. As Friedrich List, the nationalist and father of German protectionism, observed, the doctrine of free trade and laissez faire became —to an even greater extent than cotton cloth itself—Great Britain's principal export. President Grant knew very well why the American bourgeoisie, which he represented, had no interest whatever in importing textiles and still less in importing the doctrine of free trade.

But in all Latin America, after winning the civil wars and insuring the use of the power of the state against nationalist and protectionist interests ("Americans"), the "European party" of the dominant lumpenbourgeoisie—

producers and exporters of minerals and agricultural and livestock products—welcomed the free trade doctrine enthusiastically and frequently outdid the industrialists of Manchester in advocating laissez-faire policies. They permitted the government to do what suited the bourgeoisie and prevented it from doing what did not suit the bourgeoisie.

Claudio Véliz explains the case of Chile as follows:

The mining exporters of the north of the country were free traders. This policy was not fundamentally due to reasons of doctrine—though they also had these—but rather to the simple reason that these gentlemen were blessed with common sense. They exported copper, silver, nitrates, and other minerals of lesser importance to Europe and the United States, where they were paid in pounds sterling or dollars. With this money they bought equipment, machinery, manufactures, or high quality consumer goods at very low prices. It is hard to conceive of an altruism or a farsighted or prophetic vision which would lead these exporters to pay export and import duties with a view to the possible industrialization of the country. Tied to the liberal ideas of the era, they would have argued that if it were really worthwhile developing Chilean industry, this should at least be efficient enough to compete with European industry, which had to pay high freight charges before reaching our shores. . . . The agricultural and livestock exporters of the South were also emphatically free traders. . . . For these *hacendados,* who were paid in pounds sterling, the idea of taxing the export of wheat or of imposing protective duties on imports was simply insanity. . . . The big import houses of Valparaíso and Santiago also were free traders. Could anyone imagine an import firm supporting the establishment of high import duties to protect national industry! . . . Here, then, is the powerful coalition of strong interests, which dominated the economic policy of Chile during the past century and part of the present century. None of the three had the least interest in a policy of protectionism (Véliz 1963: 237–239).

Argentina experienced a similar process, as Aldo Ferrer explains:

> The merchants and livestock owners, who were the dynamic forces in the development of the littoral, were chiefly interested in the expansion of exports. Free trade thus became the philosophy and practical policy of these groups. . . . Free exports also meant freedom to import (Ferrer, 1967: 56).

This caused a constant pressure on the balance of payments which in turn led to repeated devaluations of the currency.

> Because the livestock industry . . . was conducted principally in large properties belonging to few owners and because commercial activity was dominated by a few groups connected with foreign trade, income was concentrated in a small part of the population—cattle raisers and merchants. . . . After Independence, government deficits and the issue of paper money led to currency depreciations. . . . The wages of agricultural and urban workers went up less than the general price level, which was closely tied to export prices and to the prices of imports required for domestic consumption. . . . As the peso depreciated, the domestic price of exports increased, raising the price of internal consumption of livestock products. Domestic prices of imports also went up proportionately to the depreciation of the currency. . . . As export prices and, consequently, the income of cattle raisers and merchants increased *pari passu* with currency devaluation, there was an internal transfer of income from one social group to another, which led to further concentration of income (Ferrer, ibid.: 58).

This class policy of "expansion of exports, by lowering the foreign price," favored the interests (that is, the income) of the bourgeois producers and exporters of livestock products—and, in other Latin American countries, of mining products as well. It concentrated income in a few hands, limited the internal market, discouraged domestic industry, and thus increased dependence still further. That is to say, this bourgeois class policy proved to be a policy of underdevelopment. If this process sounds familiar to the reader who is unfamiliar with the history of the last century, we assure him that this is so not because he is confusing the past with the present, but simply because the same process is being repeated in our time. Quoting Aldo Ferrer once again:

> In January 1959, Argentina began the application of a stabilization plan. . . . At the same time, the exchange rate structure was liberalized, and the peso was devalued. . . . Devaluation has become, moreover, a tool of economic policy explicitly designed to change the domestic price structure in favor of the export sector. . . . The financial and monetary policy . . . has been accompanied by a strongly regressive redistribution of income . . . and the *backward* structural adjustment of the Argentinian economy (Ferrer, 1963: 501–514; emphasis in original).

Unfortunately the policy of underdevelopment is not an Argentine monopoly, nor is it limited to a single period in history. The policy of lumpendevelopment is characteristic of the lumpenbourgeoisie in all of Latin America and at many stages of its underdevelopment. Let us examine another stage—the period of liberal reform.

5. Liberal Reform

The liberal reforms of the nineteenth century in Latin America, like the Independence movement, are generally interpreted by the liberals themselves and by their intellectual heirs as great social transformations caused by currents of ideological enlightenment which originated in the metropolis. However, the influence of the metropolis on both movements, while undeniable, was not simply ideological or cultural. Nor can the fact that liberal ideas, such as the free trade doctrine, were accepted and applied in Latin America be explained by their intrinsic worth. Instead, in accordance with our general thesis, we regard the liberal reforms as one more example of a transformation of the economic, political, social, and cultural structure (and of a corresponding reversal on the part of one sector of the bourgeoisie) that can be explained in terms of an earlier change in the colonial relationship between the metropolis and Latin America. The altered relationship, in turn, reaffirmed the new colonial trends. Concretely, we propose the hypothesis that the liberal reform did not originate when the new wave of liberal ideas initiated by the European revolutions of 1848 reached Latin America, or because certain enlightened groups wanted reform for philosophical reasons. We maintain that the assumption of state power and the imposition of the new liberal policy occurred in each country only after an appreciable increase in the production and exportation of coffee, sugar, meat, wheat, cotton, and tin (depending on the country) had placed one of these primary raw materials in the leading position, accounting for more than 50 percent of that country's total exports. Such a development fortified the economic and political power of the liberals, enabling them to impose liberal policies at the very time when their interest in doing so had increased. To confirm, disprove, or modify the hypothesis, it would be necessary to investigate and interpret the dates of the liberal governments, the booms and changes in production for export, and the resulting structural changes; it would be necessary to study the interrelationship of these factors. This is not the place for such an investigation, but we will suggest a few tentative ideas.

In Argentina, liberalism could be dated from the Mitre government of 1862, but the true upsurge of liberalism did not begin until the unification of the country under the hegemony of the Rio de la Plata region in the Roca period after 1880 and, to an even greater extent, under Pellegrini after 1890. The great boom in exports had barely begun in 1860 and had accelerated after the period 1870–1880. In Brazil, the beginning of liberalism probably dates from the abolition of slavery and the establishment of the Republic in 1888 and 1889. This coincided with the coffee boom and the growth of São Paulo in the 1880s and 1890s. In Cuba, which was still a colonial country, liberalism probably began with the frustrated independence movement of 1868 or the independence which was won but subverted in the years from 1895 to 1898. In Chile, the revolutions of 1851 and 1859 were formally suppressed, but after 1860 liberalism was imposed to the benefit of the new farming class in the south and the miners in the north—after the rapid growth of copper and wheat production which tripled Chilean exports between 1844 and 1860. The increase in wheat production was stimulated by the growth of demand for wheat in California and Australia, following the discovery of gold in 1848 and 1851.

In Central America, the increase in Guatemalan coffee

production began in 1856; by 1875 it was the principal export. The liberal revolution in that country began in the years 1871 to 1873. In San Salvador, coffee became the principal export in 1880 and the liberal revolution took place in 1885. In Costa Rica, coffee had become the main export before 1860 and the liberal dictatorship began in 1858 and lasted until 1867. Coffee never became the prime export crop in Honduras, and there the attempted liberal revolution failed. When it did occur, in 1876, its scope was very limited. In Nicaragua, the problem of the Canal arose much later and the liberal revolution took place in 1892. (For a more detailed discussion see Torres Rivas 1968: 21–49.)

Other cases are more difficult to interpret. In Peru, a liberal reform associated with Castillo and apparently linked to the boom in guano and cotton began in the 1860s, but it was aborted by the War of the Pacific in the following decade. In Ecuador, liberal reform was established after 1895 by the government of Eloy Alfaro, a very advanced leader for his time. In Venezuela, the spokesman for liberalism after 1870 was Guzmán Elenco. In Colombia, the movement is clearly linked to the growth of coffee production, but it never achieved the importance it had in other countries. In Mexico, the liberal reform represented by Comonfort and Benito Juárez in 1857 appears to have been preceded by a rise in the prices of agricultural products after 1851 and an increase in exports from 1849 to 1851. The latter may be measured by the tonnage sailing from Veracruz and especially from Tampico, the port which served the central and northern regions of the country. However, it is possible that true liberal government in Mexico should be associated with Porfirio Díaz, whose alienation of public lands was so clearly linked to growing imperialist penetration.

In each of these cases the liberal reform was not directed exclusively against the conservative influence of the clergy and its most faithful supporters; nor was agrarian reform limited to church lands. In a clearly counter-reformist spirit, it was directed in equal measure against the communal lands of the Indians. Arguing the superiority of private over corporate and communal property, the lotting of both was frequently sanctioned to an even greater degree than it had been at the time of the seizure of Indian lands in the colonial period. These same lands were rapidly concentrated in the hands of a few individuals or lay corporations—national or foreign—which used them for monoculture for the foreign market or for that sector of the internal market which was linked to mining exports, as in the colonial period. Thus the massive loss of lands obliged the Indians of Latin America—like the Africans shortly afterward—to surrender themselves unconditionally to the demands of expanding export agriculture and mining for a labor force. At the beginning of the Reform era the liberals, in the name of freedom, accused their conservative opponents of "feudal exploitation" and "clericalism." After they had reached power and imposed their policy of ever greater dependence on expanding imperialism—with the economic, social, and political conflicts and tensions resulting from this policy—these very liberals were the first to resort to repressive measures and even to military dictatorship to serve their own economic interests. Such was the course of events in Porfirian Mexico, in the "banana republics" of Central America, and in the sugar-producing countries of the Caribbean. A deeper analysis of the shifting economic, social, and political base of the reforms of the nineteenth century is not without interest and might help us to understand present-day reformism in these countries.

6. Imperialism

The way had been prepared for the incursion of imperialism and its new methods of manipulating capital in the metropolis as well as in Latin America. The liberals in Latin America had concentrated land ownership in a few hands and had thus created a large supply of idle agricultural labor. They had encouraged governments which depended on the metropolis and which now opened their countries to trade and to the new forms of investment of imperialist capital, which was quick to take advantage of the new conditions.

The demand for raw materials in the industrial countries and the lure of the profits to be earned by producing and exporting them attracted native capital, both private and public, into the expansion of the infrastructure which the increased production required. In Brazil, Argentina, Paraguay, Chile, Guatemala, and Mexico (countries whose cases the author is familiar with, although it is probably true in others as well), the first railroads were built with national capital. The railroads gave Chile access to the copper and nitrate mines which were to become the principal world source of copper and fertilizers. In Brazil, the railways led to the coffee plantations which supplied nearly the entire world. Foreign capital did not enter these areas to take over the ownership and administration of enterprises that were originally Latin American until they had been demonstrated to be brilliant investment opportunities (a sequence which has been frequently repeated in Latin America), and until England needed to find a market for its steel. Then the takeover was accomplished

through the purchase—often with capital accumulated lo-
cally—of concessions held by Latin Americans.

For example, the Argentinian Julio Irazusta asks:

> How was development financed? . . . It was done among
> ourselves with national resources and not with foreign capi-
> tal. . . . Between 1852 and 1890, Argentina acquired the
> majority of the elements of modern progress by itself: the
> rest of the railways that would make up the national net-
> work (the Northeastern of Entre Rios, the North-central
> from Córdoba to Tucumán, the Andean, etc.), gas lighting,
> the horsedrawn streetcars in the capital and the interior, the
> port of Buenos Aires. . . . A movement to transfer national
> firms to foreign companies began in 1877. The first and typ-
> ical case, or the model for later transactions, was the sale of
> the Compañia de Consumidores de Gas de Buenos Aires
> . . . [which was] sold to the Buenos Aires Gas Company
> Limited, along with the contract that the former had with
> the municipality of the Argentinian capital, without the ex-
> penditure of one cent. Payment was made in this way: the
> English company ordered the printing of stock certificates
> in English, equal to the capital of the Compañia de Con-
> sumidores, plus a block of certificates for five million
> pounds for business expenditures (because it did not have
> even that amount), and these were issued when the com-
> pany took possession of the factory that it bought so easily.
> . . . The only British capital invested in the Buenos Aires
> Gas Company Limited was the paper and printing of the
> stock certificates. . . . Between the last quarter of the nine-
> teenth century and the first of the twentieth, Argentina
> transferred in a similar way the Western Railway, that of
> Entre Rios, and the Andean line to British firms that, in
> most cases, did not invest more money than they needed
> "for promotion" of the deal (Irazusta 1963: 71–74).

In Latin America, this same imperialist trade and
finance did more than increase the amount of production,

trade, and profit by accumulating about $10 billion of investment capital there. The imperialist metropolis used its foreign trade and finance to penetrate the Latin American economy far more completely, and to use the latter's productive potential far more efficiently and exhaustively for metropolitan development, than the colonial metropolis had ever been able to do. As Rosa Luxemburg noted of a similar process elsewhere: "Stripped of all obscuring connecting links, these relations consist in the simple fact that European capital has largely swallowed up the Egyptian peasant economy. Enormous tracts of land, labor, and labor products without number, accruing to the state as taxes, have ultimately been converted into European capital and have been accumulated" (Luxemburg 1964: 438).

Indeed, imperialism in Latin America went further. It not only availed itself of the state to invade agriculture, it took over nearly all economic and political institutions to incorporate the entire economy into the imperialist system. The latifundia grew at a pace and to proportions unknown in all previous history, especially in Argentina, Uruguay, Brazil, Cuba, Mexico, and Central America. With the aid of the Latin American governments, foreigners came to own—usually for next to nothing—immense tracts of land. And where they did not get the land, they got its products anyway because the metropolis also took over and monopolized the merchandising of agricultural—and most other—products. The metropolis took over Latin American mines and expanded their output, sometimes exhausting irreplaceable resources, such as the Chilean nitrates, in a few years. To get these raw materials out of Latin America and to get its equipment and goods in, the metropolis stimulated the construction of ports and railroads and, to service all this, public utilities. The railroad network and electric grid, far from being grid-like, was

ray-like and connected the hinterland of each country—
and sometimes of several countries—with the port of entry
and exit, which was in turn connected to the metropolis.
Today, fourscore years later, much of this export-import
pattern still remains, in part because the railroad right-of-
way is still laid out in that manner and, more importantly,
because the metropolitan-oriented urban, economic, and
political development which nineteenth-century imperialism generated in Latin America gave rise to vested interests which, with metropolitan support, managed to maintain and expand this development of Latin American
underdevelopment during the twentieth century.

Implanted in the colonial epoch and deepened in the
free trade era, the structure of underdevelopment was con-
solidated in Latin America by nineteenth-century imperialist trade and finance. Latin America was converted into
a primary monoproduct export economy, with its latifundia and expropriated rural proletariat (or even lumpenpro-
letariat) exploited by a satellized bourgeoisie acting
through the corrupt state of a non-country: "Barbarous
Mexico" (as Turner calls it), the "Banana republics" of
Central America (which are not company stores but "company countries"), "The Inexorable Evolution of the Latifundium: Overproduction, Economic Dependence, and
Growing Poverty in Cuba" (Guerra y Sánchez), "British
Argentina," and "Pathological Chile," about which the
historian Francisco Encina, in his *Nuestra Inferioridad
Económica. Su Causas y Consecuencias*, wrote in 1912:

> The foreign merchant strangled our commercial initiative
> abroad, and at home he eliminated us from international
> trade. . . . The same thing has happened in our extractive
> industries. The foreigner owns two-thirds of our nitrate pro-
> duction and continues to acquire our most valuable copper
> deposits. The merchant marine . . . has fallen into sad

straits and continues to cede ground to foreign shipping even in the coastwise trade. The majority of the insurance companies that operate among us have their head offices abroad. The national banks have ceded and keep ceding ground to the branches of foreign banks. An ever growing share of the bonds of savings institutions are passing into the hands of foreigners who live abroad.

With the development of the new colonial structure of nineteenth-century imperialism, foreign capital acquired an importance that was almost equal to that of foreign trade in the task of transforming the economic, social, and political life of Latin America in a way that would consolidate the structure of its underdevelopment.

However, it should not be thought that this process of imperialist penetration of the Latin American economy was due exclusively to the activities of the metropolis. The participation and cooperation of the Latin American bourgeoisie was equally responsible. In this period, as it had been earlier and would be again, the class policy of the local bourgeoisie served to accelerate the penetration, strengthen dependence, and deepen underdevelopment in Latin America. In his study made in the Mexican state of San Luis Potosí, James D. Cockcroft says:

> In San Luis Potosí a handful of elite families, often in cooperation with foreign businessmen, dominated economic, political, and social life. A system of interlocking economic interests between city, mine, and farm, tending toward increased industrialization, monopolization, mechanization, profit-making, and participation of foreign capital, resulted in significant changes throughout the state's social structure. . . .
>
> Foreign economic investments were often encouraged and abetted by local businessmen of elite families, who welcomed new railroads to market their minerals and agricul-

tural produce. In addition, a shrewd San Luis Potosí businessman who could wangle a railroad concession out of the federal government might sell it at a handsome profit to American investors. This is precisely what Governor Pedro Díez Gutiérrez did in 1888. . . . Ignoring blueprints for running the line all the way to Río Verde, American engineers completed the shorter and cheaper link from Matehuala's mines to the north-south trunk line connecting Laredo (Texas) and Mexico City. President Díaz officially inaugurated the trunk line. . . .

Families of landed wealth . . . were quite conscious of the new economic opportunities opening up with the inflow of U.S. capital and the completion of railroads and roads across the state. It was no coincidence that the first promotional organization of industrialists in San Luís Potosí was founded (May 27, 1905) as an agricultural and industrial center—the Centro Agrícola e Industrial Potosino. . . . Its board of directors was composed of big landowners and cattlemen . . . mining figures and industrialists. Two of the state's biggest *latifundios* . . . were well represented. . . .

The new agrarian-industrial Centro welcomed such U.S. investment in local industry as the Guggenheim foundries (Cockcroft 1968: 13–14, 17, 25–26).

José Luis Ceceña confirms that the policies of underdevelopment promoted by the Mexican bourgeoisie, whose interests they had served, soon became the rule throughout Mexico and strengthened the ties of dependence.

During the period of General Porfirio Díaz (1876–1911) foreign capital penetrated deeply in the Mexican economy . . . it did not stimulate the rise of an independent Mexican bourgeoisie. . . . High government officials, including members of General Díaz's cabinet, had close ties with foreign investors. . . . A considerable number of state governors, members of Congress and other representatives of the bourgeoisie . . . who were involved in foreign enterprises and had investments in banks, industries, mining, commercial firms, etc., were, at the same time, large landowners (Ceceña 1969: 79–80).

However, the collaborators or lumpenbourgeois agents of imperialism have themselves outdone contemporary scholars in acknowledging their responsibility and their pride in serving imperialism (as they do even now). The President of Mexico, General Porfirio Díaz, said: "Since I am responsible for the investment of hundreds of millions of dollars of foreign capital in my country, I believe that I should remain at my post until I have guaranteed a competent successor" (quoted in Cosío Villegas II, 1965: 1183). Similarly, Federico Pinedo, the Argentinian Minister of the Treasury in the 1930s, commented:

If having been the lawyer for the railroads, streetcars, banks, electrical companies, shipping lines, insurance companies, grain merchants, and great industrial and financial consortia established in this country by Argentinians and foreigners constitutes treason, then prominent Argentinians of an earlier generation, who had been professional consultants to these same enterprises and to whom monuments have been erected in commemoration of their services to their country, are also traitors. Almost all the enterprises which it has been my pleasure to sponsor or advise in a professional capacity, at one time or another, were, at one time or another, clients of my father's firm; and he was a partner of Argentinian presidents: Pellegrini and Sáenz Peña [in the early 1900s]. Or they were the clients of other prominent lawyers of that era—Rosa or Romero, Lucio or Alberto López, Julio García or Enrique García Merou, as, a generation before, they had been clients of my grandfather, whose name I bear, or of his friend and relative Don Bernardo de Irigoyen, or of Quintana or Domínguez or Ugarte (quoted in Parera Dennis, 1964: 14).

Will his sons, grandsons, friends, and relations also be "celebrated . . . for distinguished services to their country"?

7. Bourgeois Nationalism

In Latin America, World War I gave the satellite economies a respite from foreign trade and foreign capital, as well as from other ties with the metropolis. Accordingly, as had happened before and would again, Latin Americans undertook their own industrial development, primarily for the internal consumer-goods market. But immediately after the war ended, the industry of the metropolis, now increasingly based in the United States, expanded into precisely those regions and sectors—especially consumer-goods production in Buenos Aires and São Paulo—which Latin Americans had recently opened up industrially and shown to be profitable. Here, supported by their financial, technological, and political power, the giant American and British corporations displaced and even replaced (that is, de-patriated) Latin American industry. The balance of payments crises that naturally followed were met by foreign loans to cover the Latin American deficits and to extract government concessions for increased penetration of the Latin American economies by the metropolis.

The 1929 crash, contrary to international trade theory but true to historical precedent, sharply reduced foreign capital as well as foreign trade. As a result, the transfer of satellite investment resources to the metropolis was also reduced. This weakening of economic ties with Latin America and the reduction of metropolitan political interference in the area began during the depression of 1930, was maintained by the recession of 1937, and was continued by World War II and its aftermath of reconstruction until the early 1950s. It created economic conditions and permitted political changes in Latin America which

75

resulted in the beginning of the area's strongest nationalist policy and biggest independent industrialization drive since the post-independence 1830s and 1840s.

It is essential to understand that the recent changes in the class structure of Brazil, Argentina, Chile, Venezuela, Mexico, and other parts of Latin America have occurred both within their external and internal colonial structure and substantially in response to metropolitan-generated changes in their colonial relations. And it is important to interpret these changes of class structure in terms of the colonial structure that underlies them. This must be done primarily by Latin American social scientists and other intellectuals who have been able to free themselves from the ideological and political commitment to the bourgeois order created by these developments.

The economic shock of the drastic reduction of Latin America's import capacity and the decline of metropolitan manufacturing exports and of foreign investment and loans—which was caused by the depression in the metropolis—had far-reaching economic and political consequences in many parts of Latin America. It is essential to understand both the extent *and the limitations* of these consequences before we can adequately comprehend the resulting economic and political problems of today. The onset of the depression changed national income and its distribution in Latin America to such an extent that the existing institutional framework was unable to cope with the necessary adjustments. Revolutions occurred in 1930, or soon thereafter, in Brazil, Argentina, Chile, and Cuba; and the Mexican Revolution of 1910, which had nearly come to a halt, was given a new impetus. Revolutionary activity agitated other parts of the continent. The metropolitan-allied export interests were obliged to form a coalition with the still weak industrial interests and (at least in

Brazil) with new regional interests which forced themselves into the government. Counter-revolutions representing some of the traditional interests were attempted within two or three years, and were partially successful in Cuba and Chile, though not in the three major Latin American countries. Throughout, the relaxation of the economic colonial ties with the metropolis and the relative paralysis of imperialist political intervention (though not in Cuba) which the metropolitan depression produced in Latin America also laid the economic and political basis for new class alignments and industrialization policies.

In some places there was an upsurge of development-oriented policy; in others there was not. Fernando Henrique Cardoso and Enzo Faletto suggest that in cases where the principal export was controlled by foreign interests and (to use their term) an "enclave economy," such as that of Central America, the Caribbean, and Venezuela, existed, the response to the economic problems created by the depression of the 1930s was not revolution, as it was in other countries—or, if revolution actually did occur, it was crushed and replaced by military dictatorship. On the other hand, in countries like Mexico, Brazil, Argentina, and to some degree Chile, there was an upsurge in nationalist industrial development. There were two conditions responsible for this development. First, the principal export product was controlled by national interests, a circumstance which gave some measure of political power to a national group—a bourgeoisie that was not necessarily national, but nevertheless local. Second, during World War I there had been a certain degree of industrial growth and, with this, the growth of a middle class of sorts. That is to say, the differences in colonial relationships had resulted in structural differences, and these in turn had produced divergent class policies in the various countries. The case of Chile needs to be studied in greater depth, for conditions there do not coincide with the outline suggested by Cardoso and Faletto.

In the case of Brazil, the depression of the 1930s resulted in the complete ruin of the coffee business. It became almost impossible to export coffee, and the resulting lack of foreign exchange prevented all imports. This crisis led to the so-called bourgeois revolution of 1930, in which a bourgeois industrial class, though it did not actually seize power, rose to share control of the state with the old groups of coffee producers, exporters, and merchants. It also marked the emergence to a national role of a region which had, until then, been excluded from political power: Rio Grande do Sul, home state of the new president, Getulio Vargas. In view of the crisis in exports, the two sectors of the bourgeoisie arrived at an agreement. The export sector no longer insisted on antiprotectionist measures or on the closest possible ties to the metropolis. Instead it permitted the development of industry, including Brazilian heavy industry. This was the so-called pact between the two sectors of the bourgeoisie, which lasted throughout the depression and World War II and ended only recently, when changes in national and international conditions made it impossible to continue the agreement.

The case of Argentina was essentially the same. At first glance, events in Argentina appear to contradict this hypothesis: In 1916–1917, Irigoyenism prevailed; then, early in the 1930s, this movement was defeated by revolution and an exporting oligarchy came to power. However, a more detailed examination of events in Argentina would appear to confirm the general thesis that colonial relations form and transform class structure and, specifically, that the populism, industrialism, and bourgeois nationalism of the 1930s, 1940s, and 1950s were the result of a unique set of circumstances. The famous Roca-Runciman Pact of May 1933 guaranteed the export by Argentina to England of chilled meats, produced by the big bourgeoisie of Buenos Aires province who were linked to the *frigorificos,* the financial interests, and the cattle fatteners of Buenos Aires. The limitations established by the pact very nearly eliminated exports of frozen meats produced in other provinces by smaller, weaker producers.

When the crisis came in July 1933, the interests represented by the Sociedad Rural Argentina declared, through its president, Horacio Bruzzone:

> Contrary to what is frequently said, without any foundation in fact, we, the representatives of the cattle-raising industries, deny categorically the existence of antagonisms of any kind between the legitimate interests and expectations of agriculture and the objectives of the industrialists of our country. It is true that we have always viewed as counterproductive the policy of protectionism for a certain type of industry which can only survive under the hothouse conditions of tariff protection. However, today we all agree on the national need for assistance to new industries which can thrive by processing and manufacturing the varied and abundant raw materials produced in our country. Everything that is done to expand our industrial production will certainly help the country to overcome the problems caused by the gradual closing of European markets, problems which we also view with growing anxiety (quoted in Parera Dennis 1964: 10, and, in part, by Murmis and Portantiero, 1968: 16).

Later, Federico Pinedo, who was Minister of the Treasury at the time (and whom we quoted above on the question of traitors), provided further clarification:

> The economic life of the country revolves around one great, master wheel, which is export trade. We are not in a posi-

tion to replace this master wheel, but we can add certain
subsidiary wheels which would allow for some circulation
of wealth and some economic activity which would serve to
maintain the people's living standards at a certain level.
. . . [O]ur country has not had, as it did when economic
conditions were more favorable, the choice between de-
voting itself to the exportation of an ever greater volume of
agricultural products, while importing manufactured goods
in return, or, on the other hand, sacrificing export opportunities in favor of an intensive development of industry. For
the moment, the country does not have this option in formulating its economic policy.

Nevertheless, as Pinedo stated in 1940:

We do not believe it possible or desirable to alter the country's economic bases. We do not propose the establishment
of autarchy. I have already spoken clearly and categorically
on this subject: I do not believe that importation is an evil;
I do not know any remedy for what is termed the agrarian
character of our country. . . . We do not imagine we can
achieve a total, massive industrialization of the country.
. . . (quoted by Murmis and Portantiero 1968: 16, 24, 32,
and partially in Parera Dennis 1964: 10).

Given their lumpenbourgeois nature, the interests represented above did not aspire to more than lumpendevelopment. However, not everyone denied "the existence of any
kind of antagonism." The small- and medium-sized cattlemen, producers of the frozen meat whose exportation had
been restricted by the Roca-Runciman agreement, opposed the agreement, which protected the interests of the
upper-class sector of the cattle industry. These smaller
producers were represented by the Confederación de Aso-
ciaciones Rurales de Buenos Aires y La Pampa; their
spokesman, Lisandro de la Torre, observed:

The theory is approximately as follows: we have a limited
export quota. Let us reserve it for the most expensive meats;

that is, let us allot the quota and the relatively good prices that it will bring to the producers of chilled beef, and leave the small producers in Linares, who sell cattle from Entre Rios, Corrientes, the north of Santa Fé, and the Chaco, out of luck.

Other opponents of the agreement said:

> To attempt, as the report made by Pinedo's supporters suggests, to stablize industries which have sprung up in a period of emergency measures is to create a tragic problem for the country's future in the postwar period, to encourage a struggle which we do not desire between industry and the basic sources of rural production (quoted in Murmis and Portantiero 1968: 18, 26, and in Parera Dennis 1964: 8–13, where the question is analyzed in depth).

The struggle they referred to was a struggle within the bourgeoisie on the question of industrialization. The establishment of these industries had been possible thanks to very special circumstances; later they were to give rise to Peronism, and with the defeat of Perón in 1955 power was once more in the hands of the cattle-raisers, the big farmers, and the new industrialists who rose to prominence as a result of the penetration of North American interests.

In Mexico, it is noteworthy that the Revolution was "made" in the decade after 1910, when the basic laws on agrarian reform were also promulgated—the Decree of January 6, 1915, and Article 27 of the 1917 Constitution. The latter established the new concept of natural resources as public, national property. Nevertheless, as is generally known, the agrarian reform and the nationalization of the oil industry were not carried out until the 1934–1940 period, during the presidency of Lázaro Cárdenas. The year of the greatest distribution of land was 1937, and 1938 was the year of the nationalization of oil. Industrialization was begun during these years and accelerated after 1940. Thus it appears that in Mexico as well, bourgeois reformism and nationalism were the result of the internal effects of the depression of the 1930s and the war in the 1940s. The author of a study of the electric power industry in Mexico notes:

The Great Depression had a profound effect on both Mexico's government and Mexico's electric power industry. The onslaught was felt almost immediately in Mexico, and paralysis spread with great speed to all sectors of the economy. Between 1930 and 1932, Mexico's Gross National Product declined abruptly. Mining output fell off in three years to the volume observed in 1907 [which, we note in passing, was a year of recession which served to hasten the 1910 Revolution]. . . . Exports decreased in volume by one-third and in value by over 45 percent. . . . Between 1929 and 1932, employment in mining was halved. . . . The country was not only passing through a severe economic crisis but through a political one as well. The political scene bore small resemblance to the relatively peaceful conditions of the first and final years of the Calles administration. Although Calles himself stayed as the power behind the throne after 1928, his influence did not go uncontested (Wionczek 1967: 74–78).

In analyzing the agrarian sector, another writer notes that an important attempt at agrarian reform was defeated during Calles's administration. The Bassols Law was promulgated in 1927, then altered by restrictive amendments, and finally revoked in 1928. Fernando Paz Sánchez observes:

By the end of 1934, the agricultural situation was extremely difficult. The effects of the Great Depression of 1929–1932 were felt with renewed impact. . . . Hunger became a pernicious condition. . . . Cárdenas understood the dangers perfectly. . . . We believe that the two fundamental reasons for the oil expropriation were: (1) the weakness of imperialism, as a result of the 1929 crisis, and (2) at the other extreme, the oil workers . . . who had resorted to strikes in the years prior to 1938 with impressive frequency, undoubtedly forced this important and dangerous step. The expropriation was another factor in promoting the development of national agriculture and was to influence other areas of the national economy perhaps to an even greater degree. The resurgence of the capital market and the recovery of natural resources were accomplished in the period from 1934 to 1940. . . . It must be remembered that the government was a bourgeois government. . . . In conclusion, the consolidation of the bourgeois structure which emerged as a result of the Revolution of 1910 was achieved in this period. Cárdenas' government was a continuation of the policies of earlier bourgeois governments, but the prevailing conditions in the national economy and the problems which blocked its growth made a new course imperative. . . . This was the reason for the change of policy with regard to land distribution, the strengthening of the national bourgeoisie, and the struggle against imperialism (Paz Sánchez 1964: 63–71).

In our discussion of the agrarian structure we reviewed the change in the direction of agrarian policy after 1940, in response to the new situation created by World War II during the administration of Avila Camacho (whose candidacy for president was approved by Cárdenas), and later under Miguel Alemán. As for Mexican industry, the facts, which are common knowledge, oblige us to agree with Alonso Aguilar:

The figures on net investment would seem to indicate that the actual "take-off" toward development occurred in Mexico in the 1940s. Then, for a brief period, capital formation took place at an unprecedented rate, under the favorable conditions created by the social and institutional reforms of the preceding fifteen years (particularly in the 1935–1940 period) and by the effects of World War II, which temporarily freed our country of the devastating competition of the great industrial countries and the chronic drain of resources through foreign investment and foreign trade (Aguilar and Carmona 1967: 50).

Even in a country that did not enjoy the conditions which existed in the Big Three (Argentina, Brazil, and Mexico), the motivating forces seem to have been substantially the same:

From 1931 to 1934, Colombia's capacity to meet payments on foreign debts fell to half of what it had been in the years immediately preceding the crisis. The country's imports fell proportionately. . . . In the years before the crisis, industrial production rose at an annual rate of less than 3 percent; in the 1930s the annual rate rose to 11 percent. Currie notes that between 1930 and 1933, 842 industrial enterprises were established in Colombia. . . . The mechanism by which our country moved from semicolonialism to neocolonialism as a result of the 1930 crisis is described as follows: (1) the crisis produced a drastic reduction in available foreign exchange; (2) the national market for manufactured goods was no longer supplied by foreign industry; (3) this market was a relatively large one because a substantial sector of Colombians were small proprietors, producing for the export market; (4) the semicolonial conditions of dependence in the country made capital accumulation by natives possible; (5) with the loss of foreign markets (coffee could no longer be traded for foreign-made consumer goods), a substantial proportion of capital was displaced from its traditional sphere of operations; (6) as a result of the coincidence of a national market abandoned by foreign industry and an accumulation of capital in the hands of nationals, a part of them temporarily idle, a national industry developed, based on a neocolonial exchange of coffee for foreign-made capital goods (Arrubla 1969: 18, 15–16).

Why did Colombia and even more advanced semi-colonial countries "develop," not toward independence, but to neocolonialism and even greater dependence? As we have seen, certain Latin American countries began to produce consumer goods which they had previously imported. But this process of import substitution was characterized by two important limitations, both deriving from the existing class structure. First, it was necessary to start with the income distribution and demand structure already existing. That is to say, it was necessary to concentrate on production of consumer goods for the high-income market. Without an important change in income distribution, the internal market was unable to grow fast enough to sustain the process of import substitution indefinitely. To bypass this limitation, these Latin American countries would have had to model their industrialization after the Soviet pattern, in which the state, not consumer demand, determines which essential goods are to be produced first. For the same reason, these countries failed to produce an adequate volume of industrial equipment or capital goods (sector I, in Marxist terms). As a result, they were obliged to import these goods from abroad in order to maintain and continue the process of import replacement. That is, they simply substituted one type of imports for another, which renewed their dependence on the metropolis and ultimately led to a renewal of foreign investments. Thus the policy of "inward development," based on import substitution, faltered in the face of external limitations. When income distribution and the national policy of the bourgeoisie had led to a significant degree of substitution of nationally produced consumer goods for imports (the return of foreign enterprises to Latin America after the war accentuated this trend), "national" industry began to import an ever greater volume of raw materials and capital goods as inputs for "national" manufacturing. The United Nations Economic Commission for Latin America (ECLA) concludes its important study, "The Growth and Decline of Import Substitution in Brazil," with this observation: "In the light of the study of the main sample items, it may be concluded that no real substitution process took place in respect to capital goods as a whole" (ECLA, March 1964: 38).

More recently, ECLA offered further clarification of this problem:

> In the more advanced countries of the region, it seems that a low-import coefficient, with imports comprising mainly essential intermediate and capital goods, meant that these countries' external vulnerability did not necessarily decrease as a result of import substitution, but that it changed in character once the first stage of the process had been completed. The countries are now vulnerable, not because they are dependent on an appreciable volume of supplies from abroad, but because of the strategic nature of their imports (ECLA 831: 25).

Translated into everyday language, this simply means that the shift from imports of consumer goods to strategic imports has increased Latin America's dependence. In fact, this increased strategic dependence became evident with the fall in the prices of raw materials after the Korean War and the consequent shortage in Latin America of foreign exchange needed to import equipment for "national" industries. These changes in the characteristics of neocolonial dependence, along with others we will review in the chapter which follows, led to important transformations in the economic structure of Latin America and produced new modifications in the lumpenbourgeoisie's policy of underdevelopment. And these in turn deepened dependence still further.

The great increase in the demand and the world price for raw materials, particularly for colonial agricultural products, which had begun in the nineteenth century, ended with the 1930 crisis and revived only briefly, as a result of World War II, from 1940 to 1955. At present it appears to have come to a definitive end. This change from fat years to lean years is the principal cause of the present notorious crisis in Latin American agriculture and the changes in methods of agricultural production which we are witnessing today. But unlike in the 1930s, after 1955 the shortage of foreign exchange that prevented imports in quantity did not promote a semiautonomous internal industrial development. On the contrary, it restricted such development, which had become strategically dependent on these imports; an alternative or substitute source of financing continued industrial growth had to be found. Continued industrial growth was more than just the objective of "national development policies"; it was an economic necessity for the bourgeoisie, whose profits were earned in industry, and it was a political necessity that would help to retain the support of the middle strata, which had become accustomed to consumption of these goods. However, for the "advanced" countries (with the partial exception of Mexico, which could develop tourism as a new source of foreign exchange), the alternatives were limited and in the long run had an increasingly restrictive effect on integrated development. One possibility—or necessity (as Ruy Mauro Marini has correctly observed)—for the industrial bourgeoisie and the government was to make concessions to the mining and agricultural producers and exporters, giving them all possible facilities for earning the foreign exchange which the country needed so desperately. This suggests a policy of "stabilization" (favored at the time by the International Monetary Fund), which meant repeated currency devaluations, a fall in real wages through inflation, repression of the resulting popular demands, and a halt in agrarian reform (though some viewed the latter as a measure which would help the industrialist by expanding the internal market). In a word, at the national level it was necessary to abandon the "populist" policy of economic, social, and political concessions to certain popular sectors and to replace it with a policy of "stabilization" of bourgeois interests (mining and agricultural, as well as industrial), which meant a high level of foreign exchange earnings and a low level of wages.

The other option—an additional necessity rather than an alternative—that might have made the continuation of industrial growth based on import substitution possible was to depend upon foreign firms (as well as on national industry) to replace imports, and to request loans from the governments of the same foreign countries to cover the deficit in the national budget. Thus developments in the second half of this century are analogous to the era of classical imperialism of the nineteenth century. In our time, neoimperialist development (particularly as it evolved, for internal reasons, in the United States) produced and channeled "investment and foreign aid" to Latin America, where it was gladly received by the local bourgeoisie for reasons related to internal underdevelopment—which is in turn an integral part of imperialist development. These new changes in economic and politico-military dependence, the resulting transformation of the social structure of Latin America, and the local bourgeoisie's new policy of underdevelopment will be examined in the final section of this essay. But since this new "development" is also the inevitable result of earlier economic and political class dependence, we must first evaluate this dependence in the light of development criteria.

How can we assess the reforms and the "policy of inward directed development" which certain sectors of the Latin American bourgeoisie undertook in the 1930s and 1940s? At first glance, it may appear that they actually achieved the "take-off" toward development that they are so often credited with. But we must not forget that at first glance the "independence" movement, the Liberal Reforms, and, perhaps to an even greater extent, the growth that took place during the period of classical imperialism in the nineteenth century resembled what today we term "development." Nevertheless, although we must not and cannot fail to recognize the progress in Latin America during that period, history has shown us that the inevitable counterpart of this progress, in the context of (neo)colonial dependence on world capitalism, is the development of lumpendevelopment in Latin America. Furthermore, as it is the purpose of this essay to demonstrate, the very "development" policy of the Latin American lumpenbourgeoisie proved to be an effective instrument of growing dependence and underdevelopment. In our own century as well, the class policy of the Latin American bourgeoisie has served the same purpose: While promoting neoimperialist development, it has fostered the even acuter neodependence and underdevelopment which characterize the present period. Without denying the nonantagonistic contradictions among various sectors of the bourgeoisie and their political manifestations, it must be recognized that ultimately it was the same bourgeoisie which had itself represented first by a Getulio Vargas and then by a Castelo Branco and Costa y Silva; first by a Justo, a Perón, and now by an Onganía; by Cárdenas who designated Avila Camacho as his successor, and who in turn designated Miguel Alemán, and so on until arriving at Díaz Ordaz and Luis Echevarría. And something else that is perhaps even more revealing should not be forgotten: Leaders like Rómulo Betancourt, José Figueres, Muñoz Marín, Arévalo, Haya de la Torre (who never actually reached the presidency), and perhaps even Juan Bosch (whose style differed from the others and reflected the special conditions in his country) all formerly sang the nationalist hymn of popular, democratic development but now echo the submissive, repressive attitudes of the same bourgeoisie in today's neodependent condition under neoimperialism. These gentlemen could, with good reason, deny any charge of inconsistency that might be leveled against them and insist that their position has remained consistent with the admittedly changing interests of the bourgeoisies they represent. Today these lumpenbourgeois interests favor the growth of lumpendevelopment, just as they have throughout the entire course of Latin American history.

It is therefore important to understand the limitations as well as the achievements of this period, since some of the major political problems of the present derive from the survival of this deformed offspring and from the efforts of certain people to produce another similar descendant.

This industrial development, this bourgeois nationalism, this alliance of the working class with elements of the national bourgeoisie in opposition to imperialism and the interests of Latin American exporters, along with the attendant ideological superstructure, were all the result of particular historical circumstances which ended definitively with the changes which have taken place in the metropolis and elsewhere since the end of World War II. The most significant of these changes have been the technological revolution and militarization of the United States and the socialist development of certain former colonies. These changes in the structure of neodependence on neoimperialism make continued nationalist bourgeois development in Latin America impossible and make all hope of renewing such development in the future Utopian—that is, Utopian for the bourgeoisie but politically suicidal for the people. This is the case not only in Latin America but also in all of the colonial sector of the imperialist system as a whole. The experiences of the new neocolonies of Africa, Asia, and particularly Indonesia have demonstrated this.

Neoimperialism and neodependence lead the new neocolonial lumpenbourgeoisie to impose a policy of lumpen- or underdevelopment in Latin America. We shall show how and why.

8. Neoimperialism and Neodependence

We shall not attempt an exhaustive theoretical examination of neoimperialism and neodependence in this final section of our essay. Such an examination requires extensive study by many writers, and in recent years this has been done. Here we merely hope to place these studies in their proper context, and thus show that contemporary underdevelopment is simply a continuation of the same fundamental processes of dependence, transformation of economic and class structure, and lumpenbourgeois policies of underdevelopment which have been in operation throughout our history. To defend our thesis we shall rely almost exclusively on the most authoritative data provided by the most respected spokesmen of the bourgeoisie of North America and Latin America, such as the United States Department of Commerce and the United Nations Economic Commission for Latin America (ECLA). Indeed, almost all of the data are taken from the official reports prepared by ECLA for its thirteenth session (held in Lima, Peru, in April 1969) in order to evaluate the first "United Nations Development Decade" and to launch the second. References to these and other ECLA publications, given in parentheses, indicate document and page numbers unless otherwise indicated. The list of ECLA documents cited appears in the bibliography.

Our analysis of neoimperialism and neodependence can begin with an examination of two facts which are readily calculated and which therefore may be a little superficial: the rate of economic growth and the decapitalization of Latin America toward the outside—before attempting to determine some of the structural and political causes of the trends they suggest. In spite of, or perhaps because of, the reincorporation of Latin America as a dependent element in the imperialist system, the metropolis's recovery from depression and world crisis boded ill for Latin American economic development. According to ECLA's calculations in the *Economic Survey of Latin America* for 1963, 1966, and 1968, the annual growth rate of national per capita income has declined during each five-year period since the war: from 4.8 percent in 1945–49 to 1.9 percent in 1950–55, 1.4 percent in 1955–60, and 1.2 percent in 1960–66. Agricultural production per capita has risen a mere 0.5 percent per year between 1950 and 1966 but, according to the Food and Agricultural Organization of the United Nations (FAO), it had declined 7 percent from its 1934–38 average by 1963–64 (FAO 1964: 16). Most significant is the decline in the growth rate of industrial output, which was about 7.2 percent annually during the 1936–49 period, 6.8 percent in the 1940s, 6.3 percent in the 1950s, and 5.4 percent and still falling after 1960 (author's estimate, calculated from ECLA 659 App. 1, Table 20). Thus the ratio of the growth rate of Gross Domestic Product to the growth rate of industrial output also declined during the last three periods, from 1.4 to 1.3 to 1.2 (ECLA 830: 10). According to ECLA, this means that

industry has ceased to be a driving force in the Latin American economy; instead, it has simply become one of a number of sectors with no special power to galvanize the others. Moreover, the branches of industry whose development has slowed down most appreciably in the last ten years have been precisely those which had the highest growth rates at the beginning of the period—basic metals, metal transforming, and even chemicals (ECLA 830: 10).

Moreover, a study of the Brazilian case indicates that:

These conclusions do not suggest that the capital goods industry can fill the role of "leading sector," for which it has been proposed, in future Brazilian growth . . . the capital goods industry seems to have joined the list of "vegetative" industries (Leff 1968: 178).

Meanwhile, the reincorporation of the region into the imperialist system of development has resulted in external decapitalization that is so significant that even the Latin American bourgeoisie has protested and attempted to induce its principal partner in the exploitation of the people of Latin America to give them a larger share of the profits.

It is generally believed that our countries receive real financial aid. The figures prove the opposite. We maintain that Latin America is contributing to the financing of development in the United States and in other industrialized countries. For Latin America, private investment has meant, and now means, that the sums taken out of our countries are several times higher than the amounts invested. Our potential capital is being reduced. The profits on investment grow and multiply, not in our countries but abroad. So-called aid, with all the well-known restrictions attached to it, means markets and further development for the developed countries, but it does not compensate for the sums which leave Latin America as payment on external indebtedness or as profits produced by direct private investment. In a word, we know that Latin America gives more than it receives. It is not possible to base solidarity or even any stable or positive cooperation on such realities.

This statement was made by Gabriel Valdés, the Chilean foreign minister, to Richard Nixon in the White House on June 12, 1969. On that occasion, Valdés was the officially designated spokesman for the foreign ministers of Latin America (with the exception of Cuba), who had recently met in Viña del Mar, Chile, and had unanimously approved the statement which Valdés delivered personally to Nixon in Washington. Net external financing as com-

puted by ECLA includes reinvestment of earnings re-
tained in Latin America and averaged 10.3 percent of
gross investment from 1955 to 1959. After the Alliance for
Progress was initiated in 1961, the foreign share fell to 7.4
percent during the 1960–64 period and then to 4.3 percent
for 1965–66 (ECLA 831: 15). Excluding reinvestment and
considering only the external flow of capital, ECLA notes
that the outflow of financial capital rose from 18.4 percent
of Latin America's total foreign exchange income earned
from exports in the 1950–54 period, to 25.4 percent in the
1955–59 period, and reached 36.1 percent in 1965–66
(ECLA 831: 37). This capital outflow includes only the
profits, interest, and amortization payments by Latin
America that are directly attributable to foreign aid and
investment. During the past three years (1967–1969), these
payments have increased to such an extent that they now
exceed the inflow of foreign capital (ECLA 816: 94). If we
add to this capital outflow that which is listed in the balance of payments under the headings of donations, trans-
fers, and errors and omissions of capital flow whose origin
cannot be easily identified as national or foreign, the proportion of debt service payments by Latin America amounts to about 22 percent from 1950 to 1954, increasing to
42 percent in 1965–66 (ECLA 696: 238–247). For Brazil,
Mexico, Chile, and Colombia, it goes as high as 50 percent
(ECLA 816: 13).

However, these figures do not include royalty and administrative payments to foreign enterprises, which account for an undetermined part of the additional 6 percent
of total foreign exchange paid by Latin America for "other
services," plus another 10 percent for transportation and 6
percent for travel, bringing all payments to foreigners for
nonmaterial services (as distinct from payment for material goods) to about 65 percent of Latin America's foreign

exchange earnings, or about 8 percent of its Gross National Product. By comparison, Latin America spends about 2.6 percent of GNP on education (Lyons 1964: 63). The United States Department of Commerce computes the total flow of private investment capital from 1950 to 1965 at $3.8 billion from the United States to Latin America and $11.3 billion from Latin America to the United States. Thus, the net flow, which is from poor Latin America to rich North America, as Foreign Minister Valdés noted, amounts to $7.5 billion (Magdoff 1966: 198).

We may ask how foreign firms obtain this excess profit, which, incidentally, they underestimate for United States tax purposes before reporting it to the Department of Commerce and before the latter publishes their data. Is it because profits on fixed and working capital are so high in Latin America? That is only a small part of the answer. The principal part is supplied by the personal testimony of corporate executives and by Department of Commerce statistics. Frederic G. Donner, Chairman of the Board of Directors of General Motors, reported:

> Let me summarize our overseas record during the past fifteen years in terms of some objective measures of business accomplishments. At the end of 1950, the value of General Motors' net working capital and fixed assets overseas was about $180 million. . . . By the end of 1965, this investment had increased to about $1.1 billion, or approximately six times the 1950 figure. This expansion was accomplished almost entirely from financial resources generated by General Motors operations abroad and through local borrowings which could be repaid from local earnings. As a result . . . our overseas subsidiaries remitted about two-thirds of their earnings to the United States (Donner 1966: 109).

The United States Department of Commerce presents

the global picture in its annual publication, *Financing U.S. Direct Foreign Investment.* The table on "Sources and Uses of Funds of Direct Investment Enterprises, by Area and Selected Industry, 1959–1961," provides the following information: in 1961, total sources of foreign investment funds in all areas of the world were $8.217 billion, of which $1.249 billion, or 15 percent, were "funds from the United States"; $1.391 billion, about 16 percent, were "funds obtained abroad" from other than United States firms; and the remainder were from foreign earnings and depreciation charges. In the same year (1961), total sources of investment funds in Latin America were $1.781 billion; funds supplied from the United States were $110 million, or 6 percent of total funds; and funds acquired abroad from sources other than U.S. firms were $186 million, or more than half again as much as those brought from the United States. The remainder consisted, as usual, of foreign earnings and depreciation charges, many of which are frequently bookkeeping manipulations to disguise real profits as supposed costs. (U.S. Department of Commerce, *Survey of Current Business*, September 1962.)

This was in 1961. A year earlier, the share of all funds invested by the United States in Latin America which were actually brought from the United States had been 5 percent. In 1962, this figure fell to − 1 percent; that is, no funds were brought from the United States at all and some were taken out. By 1963, the proportion was 10 percent, and by 1964, it had fallen again to 1 percent. Thus between 1960 and 1964 the investment actually originating in the United States averaged 4 percent of total so-called U.S. investment in Latin America (*Survey of Current Business*, August and September issues for each year, 1960–1964).

It is therefore not surprising that the author of a study

of the Brazilian capital goods industry notes that "the foreign firms generally did not bring their working capital with them but relied on the local banks and suppliers. In some cases, foreign firms also built their factories with resources from the domestic economy" (Leff 1968: 26). This author also emphasizes the fact that these enterprises established their factories with "equipment available to the firm at an opportunity cost little higher than its scrap value," a matter which we will take up again below. He concludes that "had it not been possible to invest at a relatively low capital cost to the firm, probably much less foreign investment would have occurred" (Leff 1968: 26–27).

Furthermore, as Donner points out with regard to General Motors, "Experience shows that our investments overseas have improved our ability to export, sell and service our products made in the United States." That is, virtually all of the flow of "funds" to Latin America consists of the generally overpriced export of supplies and obsolete or depreciated (for tax purposes) equipment from the home firm to the Latin American subsidiary. In fact, one of the principal purposes and accomplishments of direct foreign investment is the stimulation of U.S. exports. In view of these figures, which became still more unfavorable for Latin America during the 1960s, it is no wonder that the imperialist metropolis's contribution of capital is increasingly negative and the drain of capital out of Latin America ever greater. However, the effect of foreign aid and investment on the economic and class structure of Latin America is even more serious than the drain of capital. But first let us review another colonial problem.

Although the above-mentioned outflow of capital on financial and other service accounts creates a permanent and increasingly severe balance of payments crisis in Latin America, the continent has thus far managed to maintain a trade surplus of exports over imports. Nonetheless, while the volume of exports rose at the rate of 4.6 percent annually between 1955 and 1966, the value of these exports increased by only 3.9 percent each year, due to declining prices for raw materials. In the same period, the purchasing power of these exports increased by only 3.3 percent annually, due to the rising cost of manufactured goods. Meanwhile, the value of imports rose at the rate of 3.8 percent per annum and the above-mentioned payments to foreign capital increased at an annual rate of 8.9 percent (ECLA 825, I: 172). For the foreseeable future, ECLA feels that "the prospects of an increase in exports of primary products from developing countries are frankly disheartening" (ECLA 816: 21), and "the projections made by FAO are even more pessimistic" (ECLA 816: 25). In view of the discriminatory tariffs of the developed countries, which the United Nations Conference on Trade and Development (UNCTAD) tried unsuccessfully to lower, Latin American manufactured exports have only increased from 3 percent of total exports in 1955–57 to 5 percent in 1964–66; and two-thirds of this increase is in intra-Latin American trade, most of which is carried on under the auspices of the Latin American Free Trade Association and the Central American Common Market by foreign, primarily United States, firms (ECLA 816: 64).

Projecting this international commercial trend into the future, ECLA estimates "a virtual commercial deficit" of 14 to 17 percent by 1975 and 19 to 23 percent by 1980, not including payments to foreign capital. ECLA estimates the latter at 19 percent for 1975 and 25 percent for 1980, although, as we noted above, ECLA's estimates of these payments indicate that they have already risen to 36 percent of total foreign exchange earnings and continue to rise. Assuming a similar base for the two percentage calcu-

lations and adding the ECLA estimates of payments to
foreign capital, the projected virtual deficit will rise to between 33 and 36 percent by 1975 and 44 to 48 percent by
1980, and this is if we include only the profits and interest
calculated by ECLA (ECLA 831: 45). If we add the amortization payments at the present debt level, on the basis of
which the current 36 percent capital payment is calculated,
and even if we omit the almost certain increases in amortization payments as the level of indebtedness rises and take
no account of the additional 10 percent of other capital
outflow mentioned earlier, the virtual deficit will have
risen to over 50 percent by 1975 and to over 60 percent by
1980. Furthermore, all these projections are based on the
unrealistically optimistic assumption of an annual growth
rate exceeding 6 percent for the future, while in the past
the real growth rate has been under 5 percent and has
been falling. Any realistic estimate of the trade deficit facing Latin America in the very near future is so frightening
that no one seems willing to attempt it.

To determine the causes of these trends and note their
institutional and instrumental manifestations (as observed
in already cited sources), we must examine the new forms
of foreign investment in Latin American industry and
financial institutions and their effect on the economic
structure and the policy of the bourgeoisie. The book
value of direct investment by United States firms in Latin
America, which was about $3.803 million in 1950, reached
$9.391 million in 1965 and now greatly exceeds $10,000
million (U.S. Department of Commerce figures, cited by
Wionczek 1968: 681). In the principal countries of the region, an increasing proportion, which exceeded one-half of
all investments in these countries some time ago, goes to
industry. Furthermore, as ECLA itself points out:

> The inflow of private foreign capital in the form of direct in-
> vestment, whether independently or in association with na-

tional enterprises . . . represents excessively stiff competition for national investors, who have gradually been displaced from those industrial activities that offer the best financial prospects. Thus the initial capital contribution usually severely limits the ultimate possibility of capital formation by national entrepreneurs.

Similarly, the growing tendency of foreign investors in recent years to purchase all or part of industrial enterprises that are already operating in Latin America, far from providing a stimulus to industrial activities in the region, entails an increasing outflow of financial resources, without the creation of new production capacity to justify it (ECLA 830: 42).

This policy of "foreign" investment, which is implemented primarily with Latin American capital—as the director of General Motors and the U.S. Department of Commerce have clearly demonstrated—answers the needs of the great multinational monopolies, which are themselves the product of the contradictions of imperialist development, as Baran, Sweezy, Magdoff, and others have shown. Although an examination of this problem is beyond the scope of the present study, we cannot fail to note an aspect of it which Ruy Mauro Marini has already stressed and which is especially important in defining the "new character of dependence," as Theotonio dos Santos calls it. In order to maintain an accelerated rate of technological development and a high level of monopolistic profits, the multinational corporations must send equipment which has recently become obsolete in the parent plants to areas where it may still be used without competing with the output of the former, and where it will still produce a profit. This process is fostered by governmental policies which grant the monopolies liberal tax advantages for depreciation and replacement. The equipment is installed in subsidiaries in Latin America and other regions where its presence still signifies "technological progress." In this connection, Nathaniel Leff, in his above-mentioned study of the Brazilian capital goods industry, notes:

> The foreign firms were . . . encouraged in their overseas ventures by the possibilities of using second-hand equipment that was available relatively cheaply, so that the equipment part of their commitment could be made at a low capital cost. All the sector's foreign firms have made extensive use of used equipment which would otherwise have been scrapped as economically obsolete in their home-country plants. . . . The domestic firms have also made very extensive use of such machinery from the advanced countries, and almost all their large equipment was bought second-hand (Leff 1968: 26–27).

The resulting growth of the "intensive capital" of industry in Latin America would not in itself be undesirable if it did not entail many additional consequences, such as technological dependence, "development" of goods and services which restrict rather than stimulate economic and social growth, loss of financial control of the national economy, and "development" and maintenance of idle industrial installations. One example of such development of underdevelopment is the automobile industry, which we will review below.

ECLA points out, in the diplomatic language which characterizes its statements:

> Owing to industry's dependence on foreign technology and its development on what is essentially the basis of heavily protected domestic markets, the question of choosing production techniques that are more compatible with the characteristics and resources of the region has been left in abeyance. . . . This want of policy has made itself felt not only in the private entrepreneurial sector but also in gov-

ernment circles in relation to industrial activities that the governments are anxious to encourage. Few decisions are taken on the basis of what would be technically most advisable. . . .

The subordination of the region to the industrialized areas in technical matters has had a number of side effects which are now affecting its cost levels and possibilities of accelerating its industrial growth. . . .

Dependence on foreign technology is evident, not only in the manufacturing processes, but in access to blueprints and engineering know-how that go with them (ECLA 830: 22–23).

Although ECLA adds that "the common factor that explains the technological disparities and underutilization of resources in Latin America is undoubtedly the lack of applied research in industry" (ECLA 830: 24), the opposite is a more accurate statement of the situation; that is, Latin American dependence on the metropolis for design and engineering limits local demand for the development of domestic research and technology that would correspond to domestic needs and capacity.

In another publication, ECLA describes another aspect of the problem:

These pressures determine a structure of production in the modern sector which is mainly characterized by the production of consumer goods, particularly consumer durables of a luxury type. Even the relatively small-scale production of capital goods is designed to reinforce production machinery that is geared to consumption, to the detriment of a possible expansion of the capital goods sector which might boost the development of the rest of the economy and ensure its ultimate capacity for self-sustained development. This last consideration is all the more important because of the region's difficult external payments position, which limits imports of capital goods and makes their supply from abroad highly unreliable (ECLA 825, I: 71).

In other words, technological dependence at the entrepreneurial level and government policy with respect to "foreign" investment, 96 percent of which consists of Latin American savings (according to the U.S. Department of Commerce), direct these savings into channels which limit the "ultimate capacity for self-sustaining development."

The combination of technological dependence and official policy is only a part of the problem. It is further compounded by the financing of the production and distribution of the goods and services resulting from neodependent integration under neoimperialist development. In another publication, ECLA notes that

> the establishment or expansion of a sector of consumer durables or luxury goods, such as automobiles, television sets, or refrigerators—the base of mass consumption in developed countries—tends to depend upon the expansion and broadening of credit and loan facilities. In substance, savings and cash assets of various types, including foreign loans, are absorbed by these activities and diverted from a hypothetical, direct role in the formation of productive capital. The system of financial intermediaries which has been established in Latin America also appears to suffer noticeably from this condition. . . . Several of the traditional intermediaries have chosen to channel their assets into financing luxury consumption. This refers not merely to durable goods but also to such service items as financing travel abroad. The problem is not limited to personal capital accumulation. It is related to everything classified as "financial investment" and may occur at the governmental level as well as in the private sector. Both sectors may, and to varying extents do, use portions of their current surplus in loans to consumers or, in the case of government, in the acquisi-

tion of tangible assets. In such cases, what appear to be savings and investment to the economic agent involved, are not such on the national level. . . . It is not only a problem that affects the financing of consumption. The introduction of a series of links between primary production and the finished industrial product, which increases the number of intermediate stages, has automatically increased the coefficient of direct and indirect financial requirements per unit of finished product. Furthermore, the presence of foreign investment in the country which produces a part of the inputs and capital goods that were formerly imported makes it necessary to establish complementary borrowing facilities, which were generally administered abroad in the past. . . . It should be remembered that higher internal costs also add to the financial burden . . . (ECLA 827: 64, 127, 123, 64).

The principal sources of funds of Colombian private corporations are the Colombian stockholders and banks [in which ECLA neither mentions nor, in all likelihood, knows how much foreign participation there is], which had also subscribed two-thirds of the funds for the Corporación Financiera Internacional e Inversionistas Extranjeros. The private *financieras* can issue bonds and accept deposits; they may borrow up to 100 percent of their capital from the Central Bank and the Fondo de Inversiones Privadas, *the latter established with funds . . . from loans by the United States government to Colombia.* The *financieras* have become a principal source of financing for the Colombian manufacturing sector, but they have furthered the association of foreign corporations with domestic enterprises in the establishment of important firms in petrochemicals, fertilizers, food packaging, synthetic fibers, and others . . . (ECLA 827: 65–66, 126; emphasis added).

It is worth noting that these are precisely the fields most tightly controlled by imperialist capital, and particularly by the world petroleum monopoly. In comparison with

Colombia, foreign investment and imperialist control of banks and other financial institutions is much more complete in the more "advanced" countries of the region.

It might be believed that this foreign penetration of national financial institutions in Latin America is due to a "widespread regional deficiency of financial resources," as ECLA alleges (ECLA 830: 33). After all, the same reason is given to explain and justify foreign investment and aid and the "general belief that in financial matters our continent is receiving genuine assistance from abroad," as the previously quoted Chilean minister, Gabriel Valdés, said. But, as Valdés admits, the figures prove the contrary: "We maintain that Latin America is contributing to the financing of development in the United States. . . ." The figures also prove that the so-called aid of the imperialists is not a response to a pre-existing scarcity of resources in Latin America, but that the scarcity is subsequent to, and created by, the "aid." An examination of the facts will dispel any possible misconceptions as to internal borrowing in Latin America. In its paper titled *Movilización de Recursos Internos*, ECLA notes that

> certain general hypotheses may be postulated with regard to savings-investment ratios at the corporate level. One of these is that the sector as a whole probably shows a surplus with respect to financing its real investment. . . . The savings of individuals or families, like those of enterprises, seem to indicate a surplus of income over current expenditures. It seems reasonable to assume that an undetermined but strategically significant portion of savings is diverted from activities related to the formation of fixed capital into financing current operations and production of consumer durables (ECLA 827: 77).

The same applies to important financial intermediaries

and the financial sector as a whole (ECLA 827: 123ff). This process is largely stimulated by the foreign firms and their network of distributors and advertising agencies. Together they produce and sell durable consumer goods which the market can absorb only with the help of installment payments that are more extended than those available in the metropolis itself.

Thanks to the selection of technology and to the products which dependence imposes on Latin American capitalism, as well as to installment buying, industrial installations and their output also exceed "effective demand," though they do not of course satisfy the real needs of the Latin American people. In 1966, the capacity of the Latin American steel industry was 48 percent greater than actual production; the paper and cellulose industry produced 68 to 71 percent of its capacity (ECLA 830: 34); in the 1961–64 period, food, metal, and mechanical industries in Argentina worked at 50 percent of capacity; in 1957, Chilean industry worked at 57 percent of capacity, and Ecuador's industry worked at 59 percent; in 1961, Venezuela's industries worked at less than 50 percent of capacity (ECLA 827: 34–35). In Brazilian heavy industry in 1960, according to Leff,

> detailed estimates . . . made by the ECLA mission . . . reveal . . . that for most products, the degree of capacity utilization was between approximately 20 and 50 percent . . . [but] to subtract the portion of the market which was in reality supplied by imports would increase the degree of domestic capacity underutilization to even higher levels (Leff: 30–31).

To compensate for the cost of underutilization of capacity, Latin American industry—owned to an ever greater degree by foreign investors and protected by tariffs and quotas—overcharges the Latin American consumer. In 1955–56, prices in the chemical industry were 50 to 300 percent higher than list (not discount) prices in the United States and Europe; prices in the paper industry were 14 to 240 percent higher, generally averaging 60 percent higher; and imported raw materials (probably purchased by a "Latin American" subsidiary from its parent firm) were 49 percent higher before reaching the Latin American consumer (ECLA 830: 35).

It is clear that the policy, pursued by Latin America's bourgeoisie and governments, of welcoming and collaborating with foreign interests that control internal as well as external borrowing and determine the products to be manufactured in each country, is a policy which serves only the class interests of the lumpenbourgeoisie and promotes only lumpendevelopment for the peoples of Latin America. Foreign control is the cause, not the consequence, of the shortage of investment capital. The most illuminating and perhaps the most significant example of this policy is the automobile industry. Raúl Prebisch, former director of ECLA, commented:

What happened in the automobile industry was instructive. Not only did several countries attempt to do the same thing, but there was also an extraordinary proliferation of uneconomic plants in one country. In addition to Argentina and Brazil, countries which at present have real production, there are four other countries—Colombia, Mexico, Chile, and Venezuela—which maintain assembly plants and are preparing to begin production. The total Latin American market for passenger vehicles—estimated at little more than 300,000 units annually—has to be divided among nearly 40 present and potential manufacturers, while each of the principal European manufacturers delivers 250,000 to 500,000 units to the market annually (Prebisch 1964: 143, as quoted in Jiménez Lazcano 1968: 63).

This proliferation of producers and plants for a limited and protected market results in a marked increase in costs of production and an even greater rise in selling prices. There are other aspects of the problem which can only be appreciated by technicians; to discuss them frankly requires the independence or honesty of experts like Leo Fenster, an United Automobile Workers official who was the guest of General Motors' management at the opening ceremonies of its new automobile plant in Toluca, Mexico. Fenster wrote an article which appeared in *The Nation* (June 2, 1969).

I had made a careful tour of the plant. It was worse than archaic. Worse, because it was deliberately archaic, with the obsolescence carefully built in. . . . Overall, it would appear to have less than 10 percent of our productivity potential back home. . . . The salient fact is that the presses in Buenos Aires, like the machines in Toluca, were not antiquated, brokendown wrecks. The machinery there was also newly built—but not to produce. . . . I asked him [an engineer in the United States on his return home] about the Foote-Burt machinery I had seen in the Latin American plants. "Oh," he answered, "that is our special low-production machinery." . . . The publication [*Sucesos*, which had published an article calculating that all this cost Mexico $180 million in 1966 and will have drained Mexico of at least $1 billion by the end of the decade] was unaware of the fact that Mexico's plants are deliberately equipped with low-production machinery. Nor does this seem known to anyone else with authority, inclination, opportunity, or courage to speak out. . . . [Latin Americans] are completely subservient to the desires and preferences of the industrially advanced nations. Latin America cannot say what kind of equipment shall be installed; it takes what is given. . . . Thus, each tortured inch of Latin American industrial advance is actually a giant step backward.

Although the methods used to produce the automobiles do represent a "step backward," the production of automobiles instead of other goods constitutes an even more serious step backward. For example, it has been calculated that the annual value of automobile production in Argentina in the mid-1960s would be sufficient to double the network of roads in that country in five years and that a much more complete system of public transportation could be provided if only a part of this same amount were invested in buses and trucks instead of in private cars for the affluent minority (Peña et al. June 1965: 33). This is all the more significant because the inequalities of distribution of income and resources are perhaps less dramatic in Argentina than in other Latin American countries. Furthermore, the input of foreign exchange alone in the Argentine automobile industry from 1961 to 1964 was equal to the value of all of that country's exports in one year during the same period, and would have financed the total value of imports of machinery and equipment required over an eleven-year period by manufacturing industries (steel and metal products, nonferrous metals, cement, paper and cellulose, basic chemicals, machinery, equipment, and vehicles) to produce a per capita increase of 2.8 percent in production (ECLA, cited in Peña et al.: 34).

The costs of both "foreign" and national investment in an industry like the automobile industry lead to greater underdevelopment. They result in underutilization of national resources, improper use of resources which might have been more adequately employed in promoting self-sustaining economic development, deepening inequalities in the distribution of national income, and the creation by these industries of vested economic, social, and political interests which are committed to continuing policies of underdevelopment. All this has an unfavorable effect on other existing industries and on the national economy as a whole.

Perhaps it is not superfluous to repeat that 96 percent of "North American" investment in these and other activities is made with Latin American savings, and consequently with the enthusiastic cooperation of the state and private enterprise of the "national" lumpenbourgeoisie. This "foreign" investment obliges Latin American capital to undertake the financing of burdensome industrial installations which are only partially utilized or utilized to further the lumpenbourgeois "development policy" which results in greater dependence and fortifies the structure of under- and lumpendevelopment. This process is clearly discernible in the structure of employment and income distribution, which we will examine below.

Changes in the characteristics of economic dependence have caused important modifications in the structure of employment in Latin America throughout the past half-century, as well as in recent years. Employment in agriculture and mining fell from 60 percent of the labor force in 1925 to 55 percent in 1950 and 43 percent in 1969. In some countries of the region, of course, the fall was considerably greater, while in others it was less. At first glance, this trend might be viewed as the natural counterpart of economic development since the metropolitan countries experienced an apparently similar trend in the course of their development. However, in the metropolitan countries agriculture evolved as one of various complementary sectors of the national economy, of which it was an integral part. In spite of certain transitional dislocations, metropolitan development permitted the movement of agricultural labor into industry (and to "new" countries overseas). This was not the case in Latin America and other dependent colonies. There, the most significant agricultural development was linked to the metropolis rather than to the other sectors of the national economies. The subsequent development of agriculture in the metropolis itself, and of industrial synthetics, has limited the growth of demand and price for many Latin American agricultural products, just as monopolistic development of metropolitan industry has restricted industrial development and, particularly, the utilization of labor in Latin America. Given Latin America's position of neocolonial dependence in the world capitalist system, metropolitan development and the consequent transfer of agricultural labor to other sectors have created a situation in which Latin American agriculture must rid itself of economically inactive labor, while at the same time the absorption of this labor into productive, industrial activities is prevented. Evidence of this situation and its increasingly serious consequences is provided by recent studies by ECLA and the International Labor Organization (ILO).

The share of industrial production in the Gross Domestic Product in Latin America has risen from 11 percent in 1925 to 19 percent in 1950, 22 percent in 1960, and 23 percent in 1967. Nevertheless, industry employed 14 percent of the total labor force in 1925, 14 percent in 1950, 14 percent in 1960, and 14 percent again in 1969 (ECLA 830: 5 and 831: 79). This means that industrial growth has failed to provide employment opportunities to a greater proportion of the labor force. Indeed, while the metal and mechanical industries increased their share of output from 14 percent to 25 percent between 1950 and 1960, their share of employment only rose from 18 to 21 percent (ECLA 827: 45). This trend is doubly alarming because while the growth rate of total manufacturing employment declined from 2.6 percent annually in the 1950s to 2.3 percent annually since 1960, the corresponding decline in factory employment was from 3.7 to 2.9 percent and employment in handicraft industries (four persons or fewer per shop) increased from 1.5 to 1.6 percent (ECLA 825, I: 55). For the entire period, industrial employment remained stagnant at 14 percent, while employment in agriculture and mining declined from 60 percent of the labor force in 1925 to 55 percent in 1950 and to 43 percent in 1969. For lack of industrial employment, this relative exodus from agriculture had to be absorbed in the construction and service sectors, which increased their share of employment from 26 percent in 1925 to 31 percent in 1950 and then, dramatically, to 43 percent in 1969 (ECLA 825, I: 54).

Graver still is the fact that 10 points of this 12 point increase in the past nineteen years was absorbed by commercial, financial, other services, and other unspecified activities. The two latter categories ("other services" and "unspecified activities") alone account for 23 percent of the labor force in 1969. It is particularly significant that these unspecified activities, "which essentially are nothing more than unemployment or marginal services of lowest productivity," increased from 2.3 percent to 5.6 percent of the labor force during these two decades (ECLA 825, I: 54–57). In other words, the genuinely unproductive service sectors absorbed more than 30 percent of the growth of the labor force from 1925 to 1950, 40 percent of the growth in the 1950s, and nearly half of the growth of the labor force since 1960; furthermore, more than half of this growth went into the category of "other unspecified activities" (ECLA 827: 51–52). ECLA comments:

> From the body of information that exists on the subject, it is apparent that many of the Latin American economies are finding it increasingly difficult to absorb an adequate amount of manpower into productive jobs. . . . The out-

come has been that unemployment and underemployment, which used to be relatively slight, have become at least far more obvious in the 1960s. It is impossible to gauge the extent of this phenomenon from the statistics available (ECLA 825, I: 59).

Nevertheless, ECLA (and, simultaneously, the ILO, which comes to similar conclusions) has constructed estimates of equivalent unemployment, that is, of the volume of unemployment plus the unemployment equivalent of underemployment. This laboriously constructed estimate demonstrates that the equivalent of 25 million people, or one-fourth of the economically active population of Latin America, is unemployed. Of this total, agriculture accounts for 11 million persons, or 45 percent of equivalent unemployment, and the aforementioned "other services" and "unspecified activities" absorb nearly 10 million, or 39 percent, of the equivalent unemployment. Adding the commercial and financial sectors, which include small merchants, these three categories alone include 11.4 million individuals—45 percent of the unemployed or nearly 14 percent of the total population of working age (ECLA 825, I: 65–66). Of this enormous equivalent unemployment, the totally unemployed account for less than half and the underemployed for more than two-thirds (ECLA 825, I: 62).

In the next ten years the unemployment problem will become still more serious. In order to eliminate this unemployment by absorbing both the natural growth of the labor force and the already existing unemployment, it would be necessary for employment to increase at the rate of 5.5 percent each year. This would require an 8.8 percent per annum growth rate of Gross Domestic Product. In fact, simply to absorb the natural increase in the labor force and to maintain the present level of 25 percent equivalent unemployment would require a 4 percent annual increase in employment, which means a 6.5 percent rate of growth of Gross Domestic Product in the 1970s (ECLA 836: 34–35).

To appreciate the meaning of this fact, it should be recalled that during the 1960s the growth rate of GDP was only 4.7 percent, and that since the end of World War II this rate has tended to go steadily downward. The present growth rate is achieved with a level of gross investment of 16 to 17 percent of GDP and has remained at this level for many years. Just to achieve a 7 percent growth rate of GDP, which would merely maintain the present level of unemployment (and, as ECLA notes, would nonetheless dangerously increase the commercial gap), requires an immediate increase of gross investment of 20 to 23 percent— or more—of GDP (ECLA 836: 35). This is clearly impossible with the present unequal distribution of income (which grows more rather than less inequitable). This is the next problem we must examine. It is certain that the problem of unemployment and all its social and political consequences will inevitably grow to still vaster proportions in the coming decade unless there is a total change in the colonial and class structure in Latin America. Cuba is the only country in the Western Hemisphere that has succeeded in eliminating unemployment.

The distribution of income and other sociocultural characteristics should not be confused with class structure, as it often is in Anglo-Saxon social science. Income distribution is the result of class structure and policy, just as the latter is the result of the colonial structure. Nevertheless, as the class structure and class-determined policies reinforce the colonial structure, so income distribution in turn reinforces the class structure. From the earliest days of the

Spanish colonial period, the economic and class structure
determined great inequalities in the distribution of income
at home, which severely limited the internal market and
led the Latin American bourgeoisie to invest the surplus
expropriated from the rural, mining, and urban workers in
the strengthening of colonial ties to the metropolis,
thereby promoting underdevelopment. The same basic
mechanism still operates in Latin America—or the mechanism renewed its operations after the imperialist metropolis recovered from the slump in the development process
(which produced relative equality of income distribution
in the principal Latin American countries) in the period
from the depression to the Korean war.

The inequalities of income distribution in Latin America are much greater than in the developed capitalist
countries or in the socialist countries. According to estimates for 1965, 20 percent of the population receives only
3 percent of all income, or an average of $60 per year in
1960 prices. The poorest 50 percent of the population receives 13 percent of the income, or an average of $100 per
year (in El Salvador and Brazil, $.15 and $.20 a day). The
richest 20 percent of the population receives 63 percent of
the national income, and the richest 5 percent among these
receive 33 percent, or more than half of that income; while
the richest 1 percent of the population receives more than
half of that, or 17 percent of national income. Thus 1 percent of the population of Latin America receives about
one and one-third (133 percent) as much income as 50 percent of the population, or the poorest half of all Latin
Americans. By comparison, the poorest half of all United
States citizens receives 24 percent, or nearly twice as much
relative income (and, of course, several times more absolute purchasing power), while the richest 20 percent re-

ceives 45 percent of U.S. national income, or two-thirds the share of Latin Americans (ECLA DI: 160–161). Furthermore, part of the poorest group in the United States is there only temporarily, due to cyclical unemployment, while the Latin American poor are in permanent poverty because of structural unemployment, underemployment, or low productivity employment. Forty percent, or 100 million people, are permanently without the minimum income necessary for "minimum access to the possibilities offered by contemporary civilized life in Latin America" (ECLA 827: 65–67).

Furthermore, as a result of the growing structural underemployment discussed above, income distribution is becoming increasingly unequal. Few studies of this problem have been made, not because they would be difficult, but possibly because they would be alarming and politically troublesome. The recent growth of the Latin American middle class has been widely heralded as a socially and economically democratic development. But let us examine the sources of their increased share of the national income. In Mexico between 1950 and 1963, the share of the richest 20 percent of the population dropped from 60 to 58.5 percent of the Mexican national income. But, according to ECLA, "the apparent decline in 1963 may be exaggerated" because of peculiarities of Mexican income-reporting procedures, which result in under-reporting of high incomes (ECLA DI: 103n). Thus the richest 20 percent experienced a reduction of 1 percent, at most, of their share of national income. At the same time, the share of the poorest 50 percent fell from 18.1 percent to 15.4 percent, or nearly 3 percentage points. The income of the lowest 20 percent of these declined from 6.1 percent to 3.6 percent—by nearly half of their previous share of income

(ECLA DI: 107). In 1963, for these poorest Mexicans, not only their relative but also their absolute income was appreciably lower than in 1950 (ECLA DI: 110).

The real source of the larger relative share of the income of the middle classes is the increased exploitation—relative and absolute—of the poorest members of Latin American society. In Brazil, with nearly one-third of the continent's population, the inequalities of income distribution are considerably greater than those in Latin America in general and very much greater than those in Mexico, where the Revolution did result in a somewhat more equitable distribution. Between 1955 and 1965 productivity per worker rose 5.2 percent annually in Brazil, but real wages rose only 1.3 percent per year. Therefore the income of the owners of big businesses rose at a disproportionately high rate, while wage earners lost correspondingly and the increasing number of under- or unemployed workers experienced an absolute income reduction (ECLA DI: 141).

Let us consider some of the implications of this state of income distribution. To begin with, the half of the population which receives only 13 percent of the national income obviously can buy almost no durable consumer goods. Forty-five percent of the population spends only 3 percent of the income on consumer durables. Therefore, virtually the entire output of the vastly expanded (and largely foreign-owned) industrial network manufacturing automobiles, refrigerators, vacuum cleaners, etc. is destined for 5 percent of the population of Latin America (ECLA 827: 46n). No wonder this industry is highly inefficient and stands half-idle.

Thus, in a vicious circle—or, rather, in a vicious spiral of underdevelopment—income distribution does not stimulate savings (ECLA DI: 33), for even the savings of the smallest sector are too high to be absorbed. Instead it stimulates the consumption of luxury consumer goods, housing, and foreign travel. Consequently, foreign and domestic private enterprise channels Latin American savings into the production of these luxury consumer goods for the benefit of an infinitesimal part of the population and tends to invest in expanding a capital goods and equipment industry which is designed to support this durable consumer goods industry rather than to be a force for economic development. For this reason ECLA maintains that the industrial sector as a whole is no longer a dynamic factor in the Latin American economy.

This process is doubly reinforced. One support is provided by the imperialist metropolis's neocolonial determination of Latin America's industrial products, technology, and processes. The other support derives from the fact that the very same productive processes and structure which promote underdevelopment also produce the high incomes of the Latin American bourgeoisie. Throughout Latin American history, the property which has produced the high incomes of the bourgeoisie has not been concentrated exclusively in agriculture, as is often erroneously believed, but also, and perhaps more importantly, in the commercial and financial sectors. The apparently high productivity of the commercial sector, which is measured by the high income it receives, is due to extremely high profits concentrated in a part of this sector (ECLA DI: 262). High income in Latin America is not derived from simple rental income from property but is entrepreneurial income (ECLA DI: 176), and the higher the proportion of national income derived from profits, the greater will be the inequality of income (ECLA DI: 174).

But while this highly profitable entrepreneurial activity at one time had to be channeled primarily into production for export and the sale of imported finished goods, it is now possible to earn similar profits in the major countries of Latin America by producing these finished goods at home—as long as this is done with imported equipment and technology, in partnership with foreign monopolies, and for the consumption of the bourgeoisie itself and a part of the middle classes. Today the metropolis is no longer interested in exporting the actual finished goods, since the metropolitan bourgeoisie can now achieve greater economic control and earnings at home and abroad by exporting the equipment and technology which is its new source of monopoly power, as well as financial control. In Latin America the inevitable and logical consequence is increasing polarization between the region and the metropolis, reflected in the growing trade gap and the balance of payments crisis and in increasing domestic polarization (which is in turn reflected in growing inequality of income distribution and increased absolute poverty for the people).

Thus we see that ever since the Conquest, the colonial structure of the world capitalist system determines economic and class structure in Latin America. The closer the economic and political relations between the metropolis and its colonial satellite, the Latin American bourgeoisie, the more the economic and political policies of the latter intensify the development of underdevelopment.

This underdevelopment has evolved at varying rates and in different forms in the countries of Latin America. In Argentina and Brazil (or, more precisely, Buenos Aires and São Paulo), dependence, in the form of exports of resources controlled by a resident bourgeoisie and produced by a labor force composed of recent immigrants from Europe, led to a beginning of industrial development when World War I provided the opportunity. The resulting economic, political, and social structure in these countries—

and the similar structure created by the 1910 Revolution in Mexico—made it possible to accelerate the process of import substitution in the three principal countries of the area at the next opportunity, which was provided by the depression of the 1930s and World War II. This new economic, social, and political structure was in turn used by the imperialist metropolis to establish its industrial subsidiaries and to assume, wherever possible, the role of senior partner of the domestic bourgeoisie, which it invariably debilitated in the pursuit of its own gain. On the international level, the contradictions inherent in this new form of dependence meant—as the statistics of capital flow demonstrate—that as the metropolis's contribution became smaller, its gains grew larger. On the national level, the contradictions are deepened by the growing degree of exploitation to which the people are subjected, by the accelerated disunion of the various sectors of the national economy (with the "modern sector" becoming a metropolitan subsidiary, like the "enclaves" of earlier times), and by the consequent denationalization and alienation of the Latin American bourgeoisie, which is sustained, economically and politically, by its "advanced" sector—that is, the sector most nearly integrated into the imperialist system. To confront this crisis, the bourgeoisie in Brazil and Argentina—and now in Mexico—resort to military repression of the people. They attempt to resolve the contradictions in the economy with measures copied from the "Canadian model of development," so named by their principal ideologist, the Brazilian ex-minister Roberto Campos. This model consists of a conscious, planned, and total integration with—that is, a surrender to—the imperialist economy in the vain hope that this will result in the outward spread of development from the metropolis and its assimilation by the Latin American neocolonies. On the sociological level, the "Canadian model" is complemented by the philosophy of the consumer society and, on the politico-ideological level, by "anti-Castro Communism" and the replacement of national boundaries with "ideological frontiers," so named by the Brazilian military dedicated to their defense. In a word, in the countries whose integration with imperialism is most advanced the lumpenbourgeoisie responds to the new character of dependence with a new version of a so-called development policy which deepens dependence still further and thus accelerates still more the development of underdevelopment.

In the other Latin American countries in the late nineteenth and early twentieth centuries, particularly the Central American and Andean nations, the characteristics of dependence (that is, foreign control of the principal means of production and the consequent weakness of the bourgeoisie and middle strata) did not permit "autonomous development" of the process of import substitution during the 1930–1955 period, or permitted it on a very reduced scale, as in Chile and Colombia. In these countries imperialist enterprises would not, or could not, undertake to produce "national" substitutes for imports because of the inability of the local bourgeoisie to prepare the way for the foreigners by independently creating an industrial nucleus or an internal market. Only after the "mixed" association of multinational and national enterprises was considerably advanced in Argentina, Brazil, and Mexico did the process of import replacement begin in the Central American and Andean countries in the 1960s (except for an earlier, fragmentary beginning in Chile and Colombia). However, the institutions associated with the earlier stages of the process are inadequate for the new period. In these countries today, the foreign enterprise must undertake to produce "substitutes" almost alone because it finds few local firms with which to associate and few serviceable plants. This is a repetition in industry of the establishment of foreign plantations in earlier periods. The domestic bourgeoisie collaborates in the only ways that it is able: by enlarging the external market for imperialist enterprises, first through the Central American Common Market (conceived by ECLA) and now with the Andean Pact, promoted by Frei, Belaúnde, Velasco, et al. "It is clear, nevertheless, that one of the purposes of Colombia and Chile in promoting the subregional Andean group was to prevent North American capital from moving still further into the large areas represented by Argentina, Brazil, and Mexico," as one of the delegates to the Cartagena meeting frankly stated (Fuentes Molina 1969: 20). The other purpose of the group was to enlarge the internal market and to attempt to make competent industrialists out of farmers, thus supplying imperialist enterprises with junior partners. This was to be accomplished through agrarian reform, which provided stocks in industry as compensation to farmers whose lands were expropriated. This was done either by the bankrupt "democratic" methods of Belaúnde and Frei or the military methods of Velasco (and possibly of a comrade-in-arms in a neighboring country?).

We shall next examine the new bourgeois reforms—integrationist, agrarian, and others—in the Alliance for Progress of imperialism. However, before doing so it will be useful to compare the characteristics and historical circumstances of dependence a generation ago, when Brazil, Argentina, and Mexico enacted certain bourgeois reforms, with the structure of dependence and the historic circumstances prevailing today, when other sectors of the Latin American bourgeoisie are attempting certain reforms. It is immediately evident that conditions were very much more favorable for the earlier bourgeois reformers, and that even so these reforms proved to be of relatively little permanent benefit to the people. In spite of the reforms, policies of underdevelopment prevailed. Present-day Central American and Andean reformist programs cannot count on an analagous temporary paralysis of imperialism (with the important exception provided by the heroic struggle of the people of Vietnam); the "multinational" corporations of imperialism are on the offensive. Furthermore, no present-day Velasco can hope for the superabundance of foreign exchange that Perón enjoyed (until it ended in 1953 when, perhaps not accidentally, Peronista policies also terminated, although his political life was to continue for two more years). Furthermore, it seems unlikely that at this juncture any bourgeois regime in Latin America—or its North American partner, as demonstrated in Santo Domingo—can indulge in populism in the manner of Cárdenas, Getulio Vargas, or Perón. Today such populism might become a genuinely popular movement which would escape bourgeois control and threaten to establish socialism by armed conflict. One year after his inauguration into office, General Velasco already feels these limitations in Peru.

In order to examine the reformist efforts of the Latin American bourgeoisie today, we will again avail ourselves of the documents produced by ECLA's thirteenth session in Lima, Peru, in April 1969. The fundamental study is called *Second United Nations Development Decade. Basic Aspects of Latin American Development Strategy.* In this document, ECLA states:

> To sum up, development strategy comprises four basic instruments of a general character: (1) mobilization of domestic resources, (2) agrarian reform, (3) employment policy, and (4) regional policy in the national sphere; and three in-

struments relating to the external sector: (5) export expansion, especially exports of manufactures, (6) external financial assistance, and (7) Latin American regional economic integration (ECLA 836: 42; numbers in parentheses added).

Let us examine the feasibility of this "development strategy" in the light of the foregoing and of other ECLA analyses and of one document issued by the Organization of American States in Washington.

1. *Mobilization of domestic resources.* Raúl Prebisch, then Secretary-General of ECLA and later Secretary-General of UNCTAD, wrote in 1963:

> This impressive disproportion in the consumption of the groups in question, and in the income transferred abroad for investment and hoarding, implies an ample savings potential which would permit a sharp increase in the rate of development, provided other conditions were met at the same time.
>
> In fact, if consumption by the upper strata were brought down to not more than eleven times that of the lower strata, the annual per capita income growth rate could be raised from 1 percent to 3 percent, and if it were only nine times as great, the annual per capita rate could rise to 4 percent (ECLA 680: 32).

But what are these other conditions and can they be met? In the first place, ECLA has shown us that in recent years income inequality has increased rather than declined. The flow of capital abroad has also increased, and ECLA projects a continued increase. Furthermore, on the domestic level ECLA points out that "the concentration of income in Argentina shows that the elimination of the primitive sector will not necessarily significantly reduce the global inequality in the distribution of income" (ECLA DI: 72). Yet the reduction of this "primitive" low-productivity and underemployment sector is precisely one of the unattainable development objectives elsewhere in Latin America. Furthermore, as ECLA notes,

> many of the conventional steps to improve income distribution do not appreciably affect the urban-rural differences. . . . The redistribution of land is not a means to reduce the large concentration of income at the top of the scale, which characterizes the region . . . [because] even a radical redistribution of the land, which would eliminate all of the really high incomes in the agricultural sector, would only reduce the participation of the highest 5 percent in the total income distribution [which, we must recall, receive 33 percent of national income in Latin America] by some three percentage points [that is, to 30 percent]. More realistic calculations would show even smaller effects. Naturally, this is demonstrated by the data about Mexico, where, after a vast land redistribution program, the structure of the distribution of income remains similar to that of other countries of the region (ECLA DI: 215, 222, 217).

We must therefore conclude that "mobilization of domestic resources" is no "development strategy" at all but simply a pious and totally unrealistic expression of faith.

2. *Agrarian reform.* This was at the top of the list of priorities when the Alliance for Progress was launched at the Punta del Este Conference of 1961. It has evidently not been realized, and at the 1968 Conference of Latin American Presidents, which was attended by the President of the United States, land reform was moved way down on the official list of priorities, with first place officially occupied by Latin American economic integration. ECLA itself has negative evaluations of the prospects for land reform, but many of them are taken from a study issued by the Organization of American States (the same organization which sanctified the United States invasion of the Dominican

Republic in 1965 by sending troops and even a commander-in-chief from Latin American countries, and which for a long time has been known in Latin America as the United States Ministry of Colonies). So let us get our information straight from the horse's mouth: the OAS's Interamerican Committee of Agricultural Development (CIDA) report (page references in parentheses).

Spontaneous Response and Adjustment

Subdivision by inheritance. Large units are protected by corporate status and liberal tax laws, while small farmers lack [protection]. . . . In this fashion, the average size of the properties is falling at the same time that the relative concentration of land is increasing (26).

Agrarian reform policies: colonization. In Guatemala . . . families, many from the urban middle class, received family-scale units in colonization zones. . . . Colonization agencies in Chile and Guatemala have deliberately formed subfamily-scale units, whose operators are forced to look for part-time work on the large-scale units (32).

Tenure and labor regulation. A 1957 survey in Brazil showed that farm workers in seven of eight important states studied were receiving wages one-third or more below the fixed minimum wage, and were being overcharged for their housing by 30 to 40 percent. Recent Chilean studies indicate a record compliance with social laws of only 10 to 20 percent. The effects of the laws in some cases have been negative . . . regulation of tenancy contracts is one of the major reasons why thousands of small tenants were evicted by landlords who sought to circumvent the laws. . . . But it must be remembered that these laws are approved with the tacit agreement that they will not be vigorously enforced. . . . The regulatory approach nevertheless continues to be attractive because it permits the government to give the impression that they are facing agrarian issues while simultaneously avoiding direct reforms (36–37).

Tax reforms. Experience in the countries studied indicates that land and inheritance taxes have the same weaknesses as regulation of tenancy contracts and minimum wages. The pressure from large landowners often does not permit lawmakers to adopt or enforce really effective regulations (38).

Direct reform of land tenure systems. The evidence appears clear that programs of indirect tenure reform have not succeeded either in changing the traditional agrarian structure or in mitigating the attendant social conflicts and disequilibrium. The alternatives . . . are becoming less and less viable . . . (41). Any serious reform necessarily includes privately owned lands in densely populated and highly productive agricultural areas. This implies expropriation of private lands now held in large units. . . . large landowners cannot be paid in cash at pre-reform prices (43, 47). The experience in the study countries forces the conclusion that farm wage and tenancy legislation, when not vigorously supported by campesino federations and by the government, cannot improve the agrarian situation (37).

Support for land reform will not come from the industrialists who are often thought to want it in order to expand markets for their products. This is shown by their consistent political opposition to land reform. A survey of Chilean industrialists found that only 17 percent declared themselves in favor of land reform through government expropriation of latifundia (Johnson 1969: 76). Thus, the second component of ECLA's "development strategy" is not viable either.

3. *Employment policy.* ECLA's own data, cited above, on past employment trends, as well as future projections by ECLA and those currently in preparation by the ILO, demonstrate that this third element in development strategy is also nonexistent. As we saw earlier, these United Nations organizations estimate present equivalent unem-

ployment to be one-fourth of the Latin American labor force, and they point out that without a 6.5 percent annual growth rate of the GNP in the future—that is, a rate almost 50 percent higher than the present one—unemployment will inevitably rise, in both absolute and relative terms, irrespective of any "employment policy."

4. *Regional policy in the national sphere.* Its purpose is to reduce regional productive and income inequalities which exceed the ratio of 10:1 between the richest and poorest states in Brazil. But regional income inequalities, like personal income inequalities, are growing. Latin America's most famous and ambitious regional development program, Celso Furtado's SUDENE in the Northeast of Brazil, has already failed. ECLA evaluates another Brazilian measure, which is supposedly designed to stimulate development in the Northeast, as follows:

> There has been a mechanism in operation in Brazil which is intended to transfer business savings from the Central-South regions [Rio de Janeiro and São Paulo] to the Northeast. It is the tax credits provision in Article 34/18. . . . Since the advantages of Article 34/18 are offered to foreign firms, the [Brazilian] treasury and the [government] bank of the Northeast in effect finance approximately 75 percent of the investment which these firms make in the Northeast in their own installations or in capital shares, all of which over time will result in an outflow of capital which is disproportionate to the investment made. Permitting the installation in the Northeast of factories and subsidiaries which are wholly owned by firms based in the Central-South of the country will probably reinforce one of the traditional factors in the relative backwardness of the Northeast, that is, the export of capital to the Center-South (ECLA 827: 111–112).

Thus we see that the colonial capitalist mechanism functions as well domestically as it does internationally and that a "regional policy in the national sphere" is as unrealistic and illusory a remedy as all the others.

5. *Export expansion.* ECLA has indicated, as noted above, that the prospects are "frankly disheartening." Furthermore, UNCTAD, formed by seventy-seven underdeveloped countries (under the direction of the former Secretary-General of ECLA) precisely to press for bigger and better terms for exports, has already failed and, as observed above, Mr. Prebisch resigned and came back home to Latin America. Furthermore, even if export expansion were to again become possible, all of Latin America's colonial, capitalist history shows that, far from guaranteeing development, it develops underdevelopment. Latin America's most important development effort occurred during the capitalist world depression of the 1930s, when Latin American exports had dropped to virtually nothing. It is clear that this is not development strategy either.

6. *External financial assistance.* As Foreign Minister Valdés told President Nixon, and as the U.S. Department of Commerce and ECLA have documented extensively, it is precisely this foreign investment and aid or external assistance which has generated not only Latin America's contemporary colonial structure, commercial and balance of payments crisis, but also the underdevelopment-generating domestic economic and class structural aberrations reviewed in part above. The more "external assistance" from the imperialist metropolis, the more underdevelopment for Latin America. Therefore, this sixth "development strategy" of ECLA is no more than the parrot-like repetition of a litany whose content ECLA itself has already discarded.

7. *Latin American regional integration.* This last-supposed development strategy is notable already for its location—in last place. For although the United States opposed this strategy as late as 1960, its multinational

corporations began to realize the benefits to be derived for themselves from Latin American integration if they were the principal international producers and traders in Latin America. Not surprisingly, U.S. government policy toward Latin American integration began to be increasingly favorable, until in 1967 President Lyndon Johnson himself flew to Punta del Este. He lent his full support to this integration and suggested that it replace land and other reforms previously proposed by the Alliance for Progress. The Latin American presidents present, with the exception of the President of Ecuador, duly rubber-stamped President Johnson's suggestion and wrote Latin American economic integration into the number one priority place on their list of common proposals. It is interesting, therefore, that ECLA, which supported Latin American economic integration, and especially the Central American Common Market, long before the United States did, now places this supposed "development strategy" in the last place among all of the realistically nonexistent strategies it can think of.

As in so many other instances, ECLA's evaluative analysis is more appropriate than its "development strategies." In 1966, ECLA itself pointed out:

> It must be recognized that the changes produced by the Common Market in the system as a whole are still small in each country, and their economies are still structured along the traditional national lines. This is as true in the infrastructure—energy, transport, communications—as it is in the financial sector and in much of the legal and institutional market through which productive activity is channeled. All these elements continue to operate as a function of the already existing internal productive apparatus. (quoted in Jiménez Lazcano: 106–107).

Writing in *Comercio Exterior*, the respected official journal of the Mexican Banco Nacional de Comercio Exterior, the well-known economist of the Centro de Estudios Monetarios Latinoamericanos (CEMLA), Miguel S. Wionczek, judges "the process of industrialization in the Central American republics in large measure fictitious" (Wionczek 1968: 675). It is therefore not surprising that, in his *Integración Económica e Imperialismo*, another expert comes to the following conclusion:

> In the first five years of its operations, the results of the Central American Common Market are practically zero. The structure of Central American national economies remains as it was before its establishment. The levels of income of the population have not risen and neither have the levels of production. The only thing that has been accomplished is to increase international trade by 15 percent, without reducing prices and benefiting only small groups.
> . . . Central American integration has proved to be no more than the integration which may exist between horse and rider, where the rider is the foreign interests and the horse is the interests of the Central American population. It is integration with imperialism, which means opening the doors to massive investment of foreign capital, not for purposes of development, but for irrational, intensive, and predatory exploitation (Jiménez Lazcano: 108–109).

With regard to "Latin American" integration, the same writer observes:

> The products included in the customs release program of LAFTA as of this year amount to 9,400. Of these, pharmaceutical chemicals, machinery, and electrical materials have been the principal objects of the 1966 negotiations. It is clear that the overwhelming majority of pharmaceutical chemicals and electrical firms in Latin America are foreign-owned. In the case of the industrial reciprocity agreements, only five of the 153 proposals presented have been adopted.

These five industries—statistical machines, electronic valves, utilities, electronic equipment, and chemical products—are controlled by foreign capital. Thus, what we have is economic integration of foreign monopolies (Jiménez Lazcano: 153).

Clearly, "Latin American" economic integration is a good business proposition for the monopolistic, imperialist corporations and a useful political device by which Latin American governments can attempt to export their internal problems by expanding the foreign instead of the domestic market. ECLA itself has noted that economic integration will not help to solve the problem of income distribution or effective mobilization of domestic resources—and these are priority problems in ECLA's view. They are, in fact, the *sine qua non,* along with the redistribution of political power, of any effective development strategy, which neither ECLA, nor the Latin American bourgeoisie, nor the metropolis can possibly offer—no matter how well they understand the problems.

Thus, ECLA, in a rare moment of sociopolitical illumination (issuing from its Division of Social Affairs, which has been the most outspoken and frank division—probably because until recently it was felt that since its concerns were not economic they were not important) observes in *Social Change and Social Development Policy in Latin America*:

> In general, it may be assumed that external support must tend to strengthen those groups whose sources of power are assuming greater strategic importance; but it should not be forgotten that external pressure cannot be controlled and may make certain activities strategic merely by giving them support. . . . [It is important to note] how much support specific groups receive from abroad, a factor which always had some influence and is becoming even more important

with the increasing degree of dependence on the external
sector. . . . If the behavior, unity, or disunity of the upper
classes has always depended on circumstances, this is truer
than ever today. . . . It is not surprising that it is the most
traditional sectors of the upper classes which insist on
strengthening the ideologies in defense of the status quo;
these ideologies enable them to maintain a pact which
could not be broken without harming their interests (ECLA
826: 85).

As for the middle classes (which the Anglo-Saxons
choose to consider the social motor of development, although, as we have seen, the greater part of their income is
extracted from the poor), ECLA notes in the same document that "the middle classes . . . improved their social
status by coming to terms with the oligarchy" (ECLA 826:
79). And further:

It is one of the greatest paradoxes in the social history of
Latin America that the middle classes, because of their historical origin and because of their very struggle to be recognized by the oligarchies and to secure the support of the
lower strata, were only able to pay lip service to a universalist ideology, while their diverse composition and the nature
of the problem they faced compelled them to be particu-
larists in their actual behavior. . . . The outstanding feature
of the middle classes and of the different units composing
them is their high level of purposefulness with regard to
achievement of their basic objective during the period of
their emergence: to ensure for themselves a reasonable—
i.e., moderate—share in the distribution of power. They did
not want to become all powerful, or to start the revolution
that would be needed to achieve that end, or to destroy the
oligarchy; but rather to enlist the support of the lower
strata, to obtain which they had to make a few concessions,
but not on too large a scale. So long as the lower strata supported and at the same time became integrated in the sys-

tem they were welcome, but the concessions stopped there. It must be admitted that middle class governments sometimes gave the trade unions more than they could have obtained for themselves, but it is impossible to disregard the fact that those same middle class governments were also responsible for the most violent repression of the lower strata (ECLA 826: 81–82).

. . . today's development leaders are constantly coming up against structural pressures, and the amount of real support they can obtain for a national project is very small (ECLA 826: 83).

Apart from the revolutionary alternative outlined here, and from one or two others that are conceivable, the only remaining alternative is the status quo and the hope that slow changes in it will lead to development (ECLA 826: 109).

Thus we may conclude that ECLA demonstrates that during the "First United Nations Development Decade" Latin America has in fact suffered a process of accelerated underdevelopment which promises to deepen still further in the immediate future. ECLA shows equally clearly that it lacks even the basic elements of a development strategy for the "Second United Nations Development Decade" that could do any more than repeat the experience of the first. Like the middle classes from which it recruits its experts, ECLA can only "pay lip service to a universalist ideology," while being "particularist in . . . actual behavior," that is, in formulating the practical policies which support the political status quo. ECLA has succeeded in developing the elements of an incisive analysis of the symptoms of Latin American underdevelopment, but the particularist and private interests of the bourgeoisie (and its ideological and political representatives in an intergovernmental body like ECLA) prevent this agency from developing an equally incisive analysis of the causes of underdevelopment and a strategy that is truly capable of overcoming it. This is because the causes lie in the capitalist system itself, and the only remedy against the causes, as well as the symptoms, of underdevelopment, is the revolutionary destruction of bourgeois capitalism and its replacement by socialist development.

The special interests created by the dependence of the Latin American bourgeoisie on the metropolis have obliged the sector of the bourgeoisie that had once favored bourgeois nationalism to forsake the alliance with organized labor and instead to support an antipopular wage policy which redistributes national income regressively, to join an alliance for the progress of imperialism (and for its own progress, as junior partner), and by this alliance to deepen still further dependence, dependent development, and underdevelopment. This bourgeoisie has established antipopular, antinational monetary and exchange policies which also increase dependence. The "Latin American" bourgeoisie supports "Latin American" economic integration in industries producing electrical appliances, chemicals, etc.—precisely the industries most completely controlled by imperialism. In those places where civilian governments lack the political power to impose such policies of underdevelopment on the people, the bourgeoisie resorts (as in Brazil and Argentina) to the military (which has its own kind of dependence on imperialism) to implement policies of underdevelopment. Economic dependence creates a class structure and engenders a neopolicy of lumpendevelopment which prove that the bourgeoisie as a whole cannot formulate a genuine policy of development because its own vested interests would be jeopardized.

Furthermore, the lumpenbourgeois policy of underdevelopment which it does favor will undoubtedly deepen still further the economic, social, and political contradictions —in short, the lumpendevelopment of Latin America.

9. Alternatives and Options

What alternatives does Latin America face, and where shall we seek a people's policy of genuine development? One answer is offered by Helio Jaguaribe, former ideologist of the now-defunct *desenvolvimentismo nacionalista* (nationalist developmentism) group in Brazil in the period of Kubitschek, Quadros, and Goulart. Now, in the 1970s, Jaguaribe aspires to ideological leadership of Latin American "nationalist militarism." In a study titled "Dependencia y autonomía de América Latina," Jaguaribe describes Latin America's three basic alternatives:

> Among experts on the area, there is a basic consensus that the present status quo is indefensible. It appears reasonable to propose . . . the hypothesis . . . that three basic alternatives now confront us . . . *dependence, revolution, and autonomy*. . . . These three alternatives suggest a dichotomy: on the one hand, "relative stability," which is associated with autonomy, and on the other, "imminent instability," which is implicit in the options of dependence and revolution. As we shall see, all signs appear to indicate the difficulties in leading Latin America to a stable model of dependence. Aside from its intrinsic instability, the alternative of revolution would involve Latin America in a series of international conflicts that could not lead to durable solutions or equilibrium in the absence of a new world order. . . . For this reason, the events of the next ten years are crucial. Only if modifications in the power structures of the key countries of Latin America, especially Brazil, Argentina, and Mexico, and of these, Brazil most particularly . . . are effected will it be possible to establish, in the subsequent twenty years, an autonomous and integrated system of development in the region or, at least, in what would become

138

its strategic portion. *In the event that such changes are not made in the next ten years, it is likely that within a few additional years the possibilities of shaping an autonomous future by reasonable, negotiable means will disappear.* In that case, the region will face the alternative of dependence or revolution and will only recover stability through a long and painful process (Jaguaribe 1969: 27–31; emphasis in the original).

The intention is obvious: to offer us a supposed choice between autonomous development through nonrevolutionary changes in the power structure, which will preserve stability, or the frightening prospect of imminent instability, international conflicts, and a painful process of revolution if we do not, within the scant ten years he offers us, accept his offer of ideological leadership in the pursuit of the so-called alternative of autonomy. In order to induce us to accept what is, for him, the crucial ideological point —as if it were the only possible logical conclusion of a valid argument—Jaguaribe asserts that we must choose between bad instability and good stability. First, he deprives us of the possibility of dependent instability, which is too great an evil. Then he eliminates the option of revolutionary instability, presumably because it is objectively unfeasibile until a new world order is established. That is, there can be no revolution without revolution, and, furthermore, for him revolution is even worse than dependence. So, clearly—according to this argument—there is no alternative other than good, autonomous stability. But just in case the reader is unable to summon up sufficient enthusiasm for autonomy within the short time Jaguaribe allows him, this sorcerer once more resuscitates revolution as a real possibility. With it, he is able to frighten the reader and oblige him to make a speedy decision in favor of his ideology and the strategy and policies of those who would implement it—and whom Jaguaribe wants, besides, to impress with his intellectual and verbal dexterity.

However, when we examine the "alternative of autonomy" which Jaguaribe the ideologist offers us as a solution for the ten years ahead, we find that his program is no more than the "strategy of development" which ECLA proposes for the "Second United Nations Development Decade," disguised under another name. But, as the previously quoted ECLA documents state, "apart from the revolutionary alternative outlined here, from one or two others that are conceivable, the only remaining alternative is the status quo and the hope that slow changes in it will lead to development." Jaguaribe himself adds that "the region will face a choice of dependence or revolution . . ."

We may ask: exactly what are these "conceivable" other alternatives that ECLA evidently does not choose to describe? Jaguaribe does not feel limited by diplomatic or institutional constraints, and in another part of the above-mentioned study, he specifies and illustrates the precise nature of his "alternative of autonomy."

> To begin, in such a short time, a complex transformation of the systems of power, participation, values, and property in one or several strategic countries of Latin America is an undertaking which does not seem feasible if it is attempted without making full use of existing power factors. In view of existing conditions, it seems clear that the key factor in the transformation of power systems in Latin America can only be the one which holds power now: the armed forces. Therefore, the cadres that must be mobilized are the progressive, nationalist, uncorrupted elements in the officers corps . . . (Jaguaribe April 1969: 46).

It seems clear to him that to transform power structures, we must rely on those who now hold power: the officers, not the people, must be mobilized. On the same page, Jaguaribe "explains" that we must

> promote an enormous concentration of power in the hands of the state, and within the state in the executive branch, under the control of the armed forces. . . . *This would enable the armed forces to assemble the structure needed to undertake a profound transformation of Latin American society. Now, all that would be lacking would be to endow this structure, in the time available to these forces, with a new spirit, replacing the ideology of satellite-dependence with the philosophy of autonomous development and to make a turn of 180 degrees in the direction in which the tanks are pointing.* . . . It is necessary to emphasize the enormous importance of security requirements in the model of autonomous, endogenous development of Latin America. It will be necessary to establish an integrated, modern system of production of military equipment. Military industries will make the same type of technological and economic contribution to the region's civilian industrial development that they made in the United States and in Europe (Jaguaribe April 1969: 46, 45; emphasis in the original).

This, then, is the imagined autonomous alternative (and perhaps the explanation of why ECLA would only conceive of this alternative, but not describe it). Jaguaribe hastened to make his fantasies (and ECLA's hope?) public shortly after the Peruvian military coup of 1968 at a meeting held in Lima.

The painful reality of this illusory "autonomy" has demonstrated that the dream of civilian industrial development, which even some popular leaders (such as the Argentine trade unionists) hoped would be permitted by General Onganía in Argentina, Castelo Branco, and even by the presumed nationalist Costa e Silva in Brazil, was in fact a veritable nightmare. We demonstrated the impossibility of success for the Peruvian version of the "alternative of autonomy" in the earlier discussion of projections, including ECLA's, of objective alternatives for the future.

Furthermore, the very first year of experience with the direction taken by General Velasco's tanks, permits—no, obliges—us to recognize the fundamental, objective limitations of this version of "autonomy" and "development strategy." With regard to "external" dependence: although the Peruvian government expropriated the International Petroleum Company (IPC), which had already been demanded under the previous civilian reformist government, this same "nationalist" government allowed the IPC to take more money and negotiable papers out of the country than the expropriated installations were worth; it granted greater concessions to other foreign oil companies; it became the majority stockholder in the Peruvian subsidiary of ITT, under an agreement that the latter would invest a major portion of the payment in a luxury hotel owned by its subsidiary, Sheraton Hotels; it negotiated a loan of $80 million with the Interamerican Development Bank, which is a well-known imperialist instrument for pumping Latin American savings into the United States; it granted enormous concessions to the Southern Peru Copper Corporation as an inducement to invest close to $300 million in increasing Peru's copper production and as a means of restoring the confidence of other potential foreign investors. The most spectacular measure has been the agrarian reform decree, hurriedly prepared for proclamation on the "Day of the Indian" by General Velasco, and the prompt application of the reform to some sugar plantations on the coast. But only six months after its promulgation, the agrarian reform collided with the limitations imposed by the class structure and the lumpenbourgeoisie of a dependent society. It became clear that it would be difficult to alter reality with the demagogy of Velasco and the verbosity of Jaguaribe, who alleged that "to undertake a profound transformation of Latin American societies all that is required . . . is to endow this structure with a new spirit, replacing the satellite-dependence ideology with autonomous development. . . ."

Even the OAS, as we noted earlier (in Chapter 8), has observed that if the objective of agrarian reform is the establishment of a new distribution of power and income, *"large landholders cannot be paid in cash at prereform prices"* and "farm wage and tenancy legislation, when not *vigorously supported by peasant federations* and by the government, cannot improve the agrarian situation" (emphasis added). However, although the Peruvian military junta has paid the large landowners relatively little for their lands, it has paid them large sums for the installations on the land, and, even more important, the landowners who accept bonds in payment for their land are encouraged and assisted by the government in converting these bonds into shares in industrial enterprises. It requires very little imagination to foresee how these Jaguaribe-style "changes in power relationships" will affect the ultimate establishment of a "new distribution of power and income" which the OAS called for, even assuming the feasibility of this "development strategy." However, in Peru this strategy for simultaneously resolving agrarian and industrial problems immediately confronted a shortage of funds, both for agrarian reform and for industrial development. For this reason, the "nationalist and revolutionary" government resorts to foreign loans and investment to save its industrial program and moves steadily toward replacement of the policy of agrarian reform based on obligatory expropriation (with the attendant economic and political costs) with a policy of "voluntary agrarian reform" through subdivision of the latifundia—initiated by the landlords and for their benefit. On the other hand, the military junta neither wants nor permits the "enthusiastic support of the peasant federations" because these are controlled by its political enemy, APRA, which ceased to be a revolutionary party long ago, as we noted earlier. It is easy enough to foresee the sort of reception the "revolutionary" military junta of Peru would give to a peasant movement with a genuinely revolutionary leadership. It would very likely be similar to the one this same army gave to earlier peasant and guerrilla movements, whose leaders—when they were not assassinated—were thrown into prison by the "reformist" government of Belaúnde, where they are still being held by the "revolutionary" government of Velasco.

If the OAS itself recognizes that a policy of true autonomy and development must be based on the strong support of the peasants as well as the workers, how can we fail to judge the divagations of "reformist" ideologists and "autonomous" individuals as anything but totally erroneous? How can we fail to recognize that the timely welcome and support which certain self-styled "revolutionary" parties in Peru and neighboring countries extend to such strategy is anything but a betrayal of the popular interest? To deny this is to reject the contribution of Marxist revolutionaries like Lenin and others to our understanding and clarity of vision and to disregard the lessons to be learned from the lumpendevelopment produced by the lumpenbourgeois reforms we have studied throughout this essay.

In conditions such as those prevailing in Peru today (late 1969), local revolutionaries are faced with the dilemma of "inside-ism" or "outside-ism," the dilemma of being neutralized or eliminated if they support the government unconditionally—as the Communist Party did in Indonesia—or, if they reject reforms which are progressive and popular, being isolated from the masses, like the Argentine leftists under Perón. Revolutionaries in such situations would appear obliged to employ the difficult tactic of supporting those reforms which are genuinely progressive and popular and organizing the masses in order to radicalize the political process as much as circumstances allow, while at the same time maintaining and expanding the independence of the parties, the cadres, and the revolutionary masses vis-à-vis the reformist government.

For the people of Latin America, the choice of an autonomous strategy and a truly popular policy must be and is objectively a different one. The Latin American lumpenbourgeoisie can only resort to military strength to impose its "alternative of autonomy" and "development strategy," both of which were devised by the ideologists of individual autonomy and institutional dependence. As they modernize Latin America's dependence by means of reforms within their alliance for the progress of imperialism, the contradictions of lumpendevelopment in Latin America are deepened and can only be resolved by the people—with the only true development strategy: armed revolution and the construction of socialism. The realities of the lumpenbourgeoisie and lumpendevelopment of Latin America force me to conclude this study with the words I used to begin my statement at the Cultural Congress of Havana in 1968: "The immediate tactical enemy of national liberation in Latin America is the bourgeoisie itself . . . in spite of the undeniable fact that, strategically, the principal enemy is imperialism."

Bibliography

Aguilar, Alonso and Fernando Carmona. *Mexico: Riqueza y Miseria*. México: Editorial Nuestro Tiempo, 1967.

Antuñano, Esteban de. In Miguel A. Quintana, *Estevan de Antuñano, Fundador de la Industria Textil en Puebla*. 2 vols. México: Secretaría de Hacienda, 1957.

Arango y Parreno, Francisco de. "Discurso sobre la agricultura de la Habana y medios de fomentarla." In Hortensia Pichardo, *Documentos para la Historia de Cuba (Epoca Colonial)*. La Habana: Editora del Consejo Nacional de Universidades, 1965.

Arrubla, Mario. *Estudios Sobre el Subdesarrollo Colombiano*. Medellín: Editorial Oveja Negra, 1969.

Astesano, Eduardo B. *Rosas, Bases del Nacionalismo Popular*. Ed. A. Peña Lillo. Buenos Aires: 1960.

Baran, Paul A. and Paul M. Sweezy. *Monopoly Capital*. New York and London: Monthly Review Press, 1966.

Burgin, Myron. *The Economic Aspects of Argentine Federalism, 1820–1852*. Cambridge: Harvard University Press, 1946.

Cabral Bowling, Roberto and Manuel Duarte Romero, Juan Escalante Hinojosa, Emilio Palma Sánchez, and Miguel A. Rodríguez Escalona. *Importancia y Evaluación del Trabajo de Andre Gunder Frank sobre el Subdesarrollo Latinoamericano*. México: Escuela Nacional de Economía, Universidad Nacional Autónoma de México, 1969 (mimeographed).

Cardoso, Efraim. "Paraguay Independiente." *Historia de América y los pueblos Americanos*. Ed. A. Ballesteros. Barcelona: Salvat Editores, Vol. XXI, 1949.

Cardoso, Fernando Henrique and Enzo Faletto. *Dependencia y Desarrollo en América Latina. Ensayo de Interpretación Sociológica*. México: Siglo XXI, 1969.

Ceceña, José Luis. "La penetración extranjera y los grupos de poder en México (1870–1910)" in *Problemas del Desarrollo*,

Revista Latinoamericana de Economía. Octubre–Diciembre 1969, México.

CIDA-OEA (Comité Interamericano de Desarrollo Agrícola). *Land Tenure Conditions and Socioeconomic Development of the Agricultural Sector in Seven Latin American Countries (Regional Report).* Pan American Union. Organization of American States, Washington, D.C. (UP-G5/058-Rev. May 1966).

Cockcroft, James D. *Intellectual Precursors of the Mexican Revolution 1900–1913.* Austin: University of Texas Press, 1968.

Cosío Villegas, Daniel. *Historia Moderna de México. El Porfiriato. Vida Económica.* 2 vols. México: Editorial Hermes, 1965.

Donner, Frederic G. *The Worldwide Industrial Enterprise.* New York: McGraw-Hill, 1966.

dos Santos, Theotonio. "El capitalismo colonial, según A. G. Frank." *Monthly Review. Selecciones en Castellano.* Noviembre 1968, Chile.

dos Santos, Theotonio. *Dependencia y Cambio Social.* Cuadernos de Estudios Socio-Económicos 11. Santiago Centro de Estudios Socio-Económicos (CESO), Universidad de Chile, n.d.

dos Santos, Theotonio. "El Nuevo Carácter de la Dependencia." *Cuaderno,* 1968. Centro de Estudios Socio-Económicos. Facultad de Ciencias Económicas, Universidad de Chile.

Encina, Francisco. *Nuestra Inferioridad Económica. Su Causa y Consecuencias.* Santiago: 1912.

Fenster, Leo. "Mexican Auto Swindle." *The Nation.* June 2, 1969.

Ferré, Pedro. *Memorias del Brigadier General Pedro Ferré, Octubre de 1821 a Diciembre de 1842.* Buenos Aires: Editora Coni, 1921.

Ferrer, Aldo. *The Argentine Economy.* Berkeley and Los Angeles: University of California Press, 1967.

Ferrer, Aldo. "Reflexiones de la política de estabilización en la Argentina." *El Trimestre Económico.* Octubre–Diciembre 1963.

148   *Andre Gunder Frank*

Florescano, Enrique. *Precios del Maíz y Crisis Agrícolas en México (1708–1810)*. México: El Colegio de México, 1969.

Frank, Andre Gunder. *Capitalism and Underdevelopment in Latin America.* New York: Monthly Review Press, 1967.

Frank, Andre Gunder. *Latin America: Underdevelopment or Revolution.* New York: Monthly Review Press, 1969.

Fuentes Molina, Julio. "Grupo Andino. Reedición del Plan Piloto Centroamericano." *OCLAE* (Lattabana). Septiembre 1969.

Góngora, Mario. *El Origen de los "inquilinos" de Chile Central.* Santiago: Editorial Universitaria, 1960.

González Roa, Fernando and José Covarrubias. *El Problema Rural de México*. México: Palacio Nacional, 1917.

Guerra y Sánchez, Ramiro. *Sugar and Society in the Caribbean.* New Haven: Yale University Press, 1964.

Halperin, Ernst. "Dangling Countries." *New York Review of Books.* July 13, 1967.

Harlow, Vincent. *A History of Barbados: 1625–1685.* London: Clarendon Press, 1926.

Humboldt, Alexander von. *Political Essay on the Kingdom of New Spain.* 4 vols. Translation from the original French by John Black. London: 1811.

Irazusta, Julio. *Influencia Económica Británica en el Río de la Plata.* Buenos Aires: EUDEBA, 1963.

Jaguaribe, Helio. "Dependencia y autonomía de América Latina." Presentado al Séptimo Congreso Interamericano de Planificación. *Panorama Económico* (Santiago). Marzo and Abril 1969.

Jiménez Lazcano, Mauro. *Integración Económica e Imperialismo.* México: Nuestro Tiempo, 1968.

Johnson, Dale. "The National and Progressive Bourgeoisie in Latin America," in *Studies in Comparative International Development* (St. Louis, Mo.), 1969.

Leff, Nathaniel H. *The Brazilian Capital Goods Industry, 1929–1964.* Cambridge: Harvard University Press, 1968.

Luxemburg, Rosa. *The Accumulation of Capital.* New York: Monthly Review Press, 1964.

Lyons, Raymond F., ed. *Problems and Strategies of Educational Planning. Lessons from Latin America.* Paris: International Institute for Educational Planning, 1964.

Magdoff, Harry. *The Age of Imperialism.* New York and London: Monthly Review Press, 1966.

Marini, Ruy Mauro. *Subdesarrollo y Revolución en América Latina.* México: Siglo XXI, 1970.

Moreno Fraginals, Manuel. *El Ingenio: El Complejo Económico Social Cubano del Azúcar.* La Habana: Comisión Nacional Cubana de la UNESCO, 1964. To be published in English by Monthly Review Press.

Murmis, Miguel and Juan Carlos Portantiero. *Crecimiento Industrial y Alianza de Clases en la Argentina (1930–1940).* Buenos Aires: Instituto Torcuato di Tella. Documento de Trabajo, Nº 49, 1968 (mimeographed).

Nieto Arteta, Luis Eduardo. *Ensayos sobre Economía Colombiana.* Medellín: Editorial Oveja Negra, 1969.

Orozco, Luis Chavez and Enrique Florescano. *Agricultura e Industria Textil de Veracruz, Siglo XIX.* Xalapa: Universidad Veracruzana, 1965.

Otero, Mariano. *Ensayo sobre el Verdadero Estado de la Cuestión Social y Política que se agita en la República Mexicana.* México: Ediciones del Instituto Nacional de la Juventud Mexicana, 1964.

Parera Dennis, Alfredo. "Naturaleza de las Relaciones entre las clases dominantes argentinas y las metrópolis." *Fichas* (Buenos Aires). Diciembre 1964.

Paz Sánchez, Fernando. *Estructura y Desarrollo de la Agricultura en México.* Memoria presentada en la Escuela Nacional de Economía, Universidad Nacional Autónoma de México, 1964.

Peña, Milcíades, Gustavo Polit and Victor Testa. "Industrialización, burguesía nacional y Marxismo." *Fichas.* Junio 1965.

Prebisch, Raúl. *Integración de América Latina.* México: Fondo de Cultura Económica, 1964.

Ramírez Necochea, Hernán. *Antecedentes Económicos de la In-*

dependencia de Chile. Santiago: Facultad de Filosfía y Educación, Universidad de Chile, 1967.

Revillagigedo, Conde de. *Informe sobre las Misiones 1793 e Instrucción Reservada al Marqués de Branciforte, 1794.* 2 vols. México: Editorial Jus, Colección México Heroico, 1966.

Rosa, José Maria. *Defensa y Perdida de Nuestra Independencia Económica.* Buenos Aires: Librería Huemul, 1943.

Santos Martínez, Pedro. *Historia Económica de Mendoza durante el Virreinato, 1776–1810.* Madrid: Universidad Nacional del Cuyo, 1961.

Smith, Adam. *The Wealth of Nations.* New York: Random House, 1937.

Stavenhagen, Rodolfo and Fernando Paz Sánchez, Cuauntémoc Cárdenas, and Arturo Bonilla. *Neolatifundismo y Explotación de Emiliano Zapata a Anderson, Clayton and Co.* México: Nuestro Tiempo, 1968.

Torres Rivas, Edelberto. *Interpretación del Desarrollo Social Centroamericano.* Santiago, ILPES, 1968 (mimeographed). To be published in Santiago by Prensa Latinoamericana.

United States Department of Commerce. *Survey of Current Business.* Washington, D.C. (various issues cited in text).

Véliz, Claudio. "La Mesa de Tres Patas." *Desarrollo Económico.* Buenos Aires, Abril–Septiembre 1963.

Viadas, Lauro. "El Problema de la Pequeña Propiedad. Informe presentado al señor Secretario de Fomento," in Jesús Silva Herzog, *La Cuestión de la Tierra, 1910–1911.* México: Instituto Mexicano de Investigaciones Económicas, 1960.

Vitale, Luis. *Interpretación Marxista de la Historia de Chile. Vol. II. La Colonia y la Revolución de 1810.* Santiago: Prensa Latinoamericana, 1969.

Wionczek, Miguel S. *El nacionalismo Mexicano y la Inversión Extranjera.* México: Siglo XXI, 1967.

Wionczek, Miguel S. "La inversión privada norteamericana y el desarrollo de Mesoamérica." *Comercio Exterior* (México). Agosto 1968.

United Nations Publications and Documents Cited.

United Nations, Economic Commission for Latin America. New York and Santiago de Chile.

United Nations, ECLA, "The Growth and Decline of Import Substitution in Brazil." *Economic Bulletin for Latin America.* March 1964.

E/CN.12/659. *The Economic Development of Latin America in the Post-War Period.*

E/CN.12/680 Rev.1. *Toward a Dynamic Development Policy for Latin America.*

E/CN.12/696 Rev.1. *Economic Survey of Latin America, 1963.*

E/CN.12/816. *Second United Nations Development Decade. Latin America's Foreign Trade Policy.*

E/CN.12/825. *Economic Survey of Latin America, 1968. Part I. Some Aspects of the Latin American Economy Towards the End of the 1960's.*

E/CN.12/826. *Social Change and Social Development Policy in Latin America.*

E/CN.12/827. *Movilización de Recursos Internos.*

E/CN.12/830. *Second United Nations Development Decade. Industrial Development in Latin America.*

E/CN.12/831. *Second United Nations Development Decade. The Trade and Domestic Savings Gaps and Structural Unemployment in Latin America.*

E/CN.12/836. *Second United Nations Development Decade. Basic Aspects of Latin American Development Strategy.*

DI. *La Distribución de Ingreso en América Latina, April 1969.* (Provisional document of the División de Investigación y Desarrollo Económico, ECLA; a revision of the official document presented at the Twelfth Session [Caracas, 1967], entitled "Estudios Sobre la Distribución de Ingreso en América Latina.") E/CN.12/770 and E/CN.12/770 App.1.

FAO (Food and Agricultural Organization of the United Nations). *The State of Food and Agriculture, 1964.* Rome: 1964.

MONTHLY REVIEW

an independent socialist magazine

edited by Paul M. Sweezy and Harry Magdoff

Business Week: ". . . a brand of socialism that is thorough-going and tough-minded, drastic enough to provide the sharp break with the past that many left-wingers in the underdeveloped countries see as essential. At the same time they maintain a sturdy independence of both Moscow and Peking that appeals to neutralists. And their skill in manipulating the abstruse concepts of modern economics impresses would-be intellectuals. . . . Their analysis of the troubles of capitalism is just plausible enough to be disturbing."

Bertrand Russell: "Your journal has been of the greatest interest to me over a period of time. I am not a Marxist by any means as I have sought to show in critiques published in several books, but I recognize the power of much of your own analysis and where I disagree I find your journal valuable and of stimulating importance. I want to thank you for your work and to tell you of my appreciation of it."

The Wellesley Department of Economics: " . . . the leading Marxist intellectual (not Communist) economic journal published anywhere in the world, and is on our subscription list at the College library for good reasons."

Albert Einstein: "Clarity about the aims and problems of socialism is of greatest significance in our age of transition. . . . I consider the founding of this magazine to be an important public service." (In his article, "Why Socialism" in Vol. I, No. 1.)

DOMESTIC: $9 for one year, $16 for two years, $7 for one-year student subscription.

FOREIGN: $10 for one year, $18 for two years, $8 for one-year student subscription. (Subscription rates subject to change.)

62 West 14th Street, New York, New York 10011